RUG HOOKING
and
BRAIDING

presented by

The St. Joseph Avenue Neighbors

in memory of

Emma Dunn

NILES COMMUNITY LIBRARY
NILES, MICHIGAN

RUG HOOKING
and
BRAIDING

for pleasure and profit

Dorothy Lawless

With a supplement including in 27 chapters
all that is new in the field

THOMAS Y. CROWELL COMPANY

New York   *Established 1834*

Manufactured in the United States of America

Published in Canada by Fitzhenry & Whiteside Limited, Toronto

Library of Congress Catalog Card No.: 62–21714

ISBN 0-690-71530-7

5 6 7 8 9 10

FOREWORD

Rug hooking is such a fascinating adventure that everyone ought to try his hand at it. You don't have to be a creative artist or possess unusual ability to fashion a pretty rug. Beginners everywhere have proved that their very first rug usually turns out so well that they can't wait to get started on another.

People from all walks of life and of all ages enjoy the hobby of making rugs at home—nor do the ladies have a monopoly. Many men hook or braid rugs and have an equally deep appreciation of the handicraft, enjoying it both as a hobby and as a source of supplemental income. One woman recently had to send for a new hook because she couldn't get hers away from her husband! Another couple have initialed many rugs as joint projects, with the husband working in all the black backgrounds, black being his favorite for setting off the colorful details of the pattern. And more and more men and women, confined to their chairs by accident or illness, hook rugs every day as a pleasant occupation, finding a ready market for their work.

Children also take an interest in hooked rugs—they love to watch the patterns grow and to be a part of the family fun.

One of the beauties of hooking or braiding your own rugs is that you can make them exactly to your own size and specifications, and at a fraction of the cost you would have to pay for a similar item in a store. With rugs completed in your favorite colors and to a pattern in keeping with the general character of your traditional or modern furnishings, no room can possibly be dull and lifeless. Decorators frequently build an entire color scheme around a handmade rug, such is the important place they often occupy.

While some bought patterns may not be of especially good design, there is usually something pretty in every finished hooked rug, for the maker always improvises and adapts a design or its colors to his own purposes. The author can honestly say she has never seen a really unattractive home hooked rug—or one that wouldn't fit handsomely into one or another particular type of setting. This is a great deal more than can be said of machine-made rugs, which lack the charm of individual homey touches. Remember that no matter how many minor flaws you may see in your own work, they will not appear as flaws to others once the rug is finished and the overall effect is seen.

If you are new to this craft, start on a very simple design so you can concentrate at first on the technique of hooking. Soon you will find it the easiest handiwork there is and will be eager to try out more complicated patterns. Then there need be no end to your imagination.

After making her first rose, one lady said she wanted to walk along the streets and tell everyone she had made it! She was so proud and happy— and had reason to be. When you start hooking for yourself, you will understand just how she felt.

CONTENTS

Part I

Part II

Part I

A BRIEF HISTORY OF RUG HOOKING

Rug hooking, although associated most firmly in our minds with Colonial America, is an ancient craft, so long practiced by our ancestors, and so much a part of their lives, that its actual origins have been lost in antiquity. The process as we know it today was developed in England and was brought to this country by the early settlers. There is some evidence that the art came to England from Scandinavia, and that prehistoric peoples hooked materials from which they made some of their articles of clothing.

However, the real heyday of rug hooking began in the middle of the eighteenth century in New England and reached its highest development there. Every well-furnished Colonial home had at least one or two hooked mats to provide comfort underfoot and a note of cheerfulness and luxury to the room. Many of these rugs exist today, handed down from generation to generation as treasured heirlooms and prized by collectors of antiques. The seafarers of that era played no small part in promoting the popularity of making and using hooked rugs, for they whiled away the long shipboard hours of dead calm under sail creating rugs from designs which were original or copied from patterns seen in English or European ports.

Early rugmakers hooked their work on backings of hand-woven linen and on old coffee, sugar, and grain bags. Their hooking yarns were homespun or cut from old rags or clothing—whatever materials they could salvage for the purpose. To a great extent they used their materials in the original or natural colors, but later began to use dyes they made them-

9

selves, with great ingenuity and no little effort. Onion skins, berries, wild grapes, various tree barks, grasses, nuts, roots, goldenrod were all experimented with and employed as color sources. Frequently these things were boiled right in the same pot with the yarn or cloth, with no separate stages of dye-making and dyeing.

As for designs, those rugmakers possessing or having access to homes where there were oriental or European textiles, chinaware, wall papers or such often copied these patterns, but in the rural areas many crude primitive renderings of horses, sheep, birds, deer, dogs, or houses or public buildings were drawn from life. Then too, geometrics such as stars, diamonds, medallions, and other odd shapes were assembled, as well as occasional landscapes. Women met in "hooking bees" just as they did in the famous "quilting parties" where they exchanged ideas, compared patterns, and shared their interests as we do today.

Edward S. Frost, a Yankee veteran of the War Between the States, is credited with raising the standard of rug-hooking design with his patterns. Retired at home because of ill health, one day he took note of a rug his wife was hooking, and, impressed with the crudeness of the pattern, was inspired to improve upon it. After experimentation, he finally devised several metal stencils with which he could stamp rug patterns of good design on burlap in a minimum length of time. Finding no one brave enough to invest in his idea, he peddled his patterns from a cart, then saved enough to start a regular business selling them.

A few years after the Civil War the handicraft of rug hooking began to die out, and was not revived again until the First World War, more than fifty years later. Through the depression of the 1930's, people again turned actively to rug making, and during World War II the craft reached one of its greatest heights of popularity. It would seem in troubled times that rug hooking has really served a real purpose other than its practicality —for how many mothers, wives, and sisters of soldiers have taken comfort and solace in this absorbing handiwork! With international politics as disturbing as ever, and the times as restless and uncertain as they have ever been, it is little wonder that the popularity of rug hooking continues to gather momentum daily.

Even though rug hooking originated abroad, praise for its continued advancement must go to America. For here alone does it represent a noteworthy form of contemporary folk art, being as much a part of us as it was of our pioneer grandmothers.

A few years back hooked rugs were considered correct only with Colonial or Early American furnishings. Now interior decorators concede there is a place for hooked rugs with almost any type of decor, depending, of course, on the pattern, color, and workmanship.

Nineteenth-century American hooked rug.

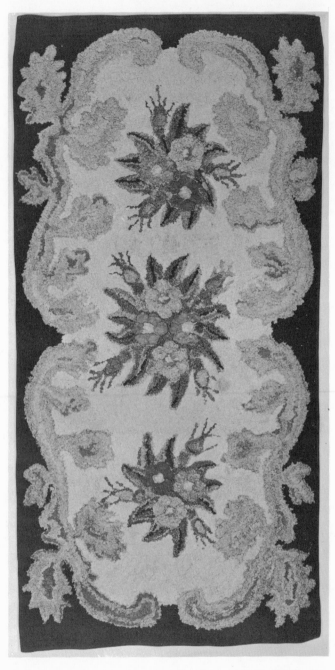

Another hooked rug made in the nineteenth century.

2

TECHNIQUES OF HOOKING AND NECESSARY EQUIPMENT

If you have never tried hooking you will be amazed how easy it is. There are two basic methods for different types of rugs. One method is hooking cut strips of woolen material (old clothing or mill ends) with a short-handled hook; the other method is hooking bought yarn with a hollow-handle hook.

With the *short wooden-handle hook* (fig. 5), which is like a crochet hook, the procedure consists of pulling loops of a *cut strip of material* through the burlap mesh or other foundation. While hooking proceeds, the pattern remains right side up, and each stitch is given individual attention. This is the way our grandmothers and great-grandmothers made their rugs. The idea is to make loops as evenly as possible, though perfection is unnecessary. The technique of hooking cut strips of material with this type of hook is developed in chapter 5.

With the *hollow-handle hook* (fig. 8) the hooking procedure consists of pushing *loops of yarn* through the burlap or warp-cloth mesh. In this case the pattern is right side down, and you look at the wrong side all of the time you are hooking. This hook has self-threading tubes containing the yarn and each loop is regulated in height by an adjustable device on the hook. Although cut strips of woolen material can also be hooked with the hollow-handle hook, this is not recommended, any more than the short wooden-handle hook is recommended for yarn. Hooking with yarn is described in detail with diagrams in chapter 4.

From the following list of equipment and material any size or kind of hooked rug can be made:

Rug pattern (or plain burlap if you wish to design your own pattern)
Rug frame
Hook needle (rug hooks)
Woolen material for strips (or yarn)
Scissors
Thumb tacks (or staples)
Carpet binding
Whisk broom (or brush)
Hammer, screw driver, nails, and screws

RUG PATTERNS

A small pattern of not over 2 by 3 feet is a good choice for the beginner. Such may be completed in about four weeks by hooking about two hours a day, that is, with the short wooden-handle hook. Yarn rugs are finished in less than half of that time. Another good choice for the beginner is a chair seat or footstool with simple detail. Patterns are outlined on burlap, monk's cloth, or warp cloth; and a wide selection to suit most tastes is available in art needlework departments in the larger stores, specialty shops, and ten-cent stores. Popular designs include oval and oblong florals, modified geometrics, and even little scenic stair treads. Store patterns are often tinted in color, which makes it easy to follow with your material, or color charts are furnished with the pattern so that the beginner will know what colored material to work with. Even though yarn is recommended with many commercial patterns, cut strips of woolen result in equally beautiful rugs, and even more so according to most people who have done both kinds of hooking. There is the added advantage that patterns hooked from cut strips of old material will cost much less to make.

Although you may tire of the commercial patterns, or want to do a more original or modern design, it is perhaps better for the beginner to start with a bought pattern, until she or he has had enough hooking experience to develop an original design. However, a block pattern which a beginner may easily make is described in chapter 6. The repetition of this pattern offers an excellent opportunity for practicing neat workmanship, is easy to do, and affords the opportunity for using whatever old clothing you may have on hand. In the event you intend to make your own design, then of course you will buy plain burlap, monk's cloth, or warp cloth at the store. Suggestions for making your own designs are given in chapter 22.

Fig. 1. Easel frame, with pattern attached by thumbtacks on three sides, and by thread laced through burlap and fastened to frame by tacks at left.

RUG FRAMES

The rug frame may be anything from an old picture frame to a card table with the top off, a homemade frame, or easel frame from the department store. The purpose of the frame is simply to hold the burlap pattern taut, and anything that will serve this purpose can be used. The burlap is fastened to the frame with tacks or sewed to it as illustrated in fig. 1. For good and fast work it is most important that the pattern be stretched tight, straight, and smooth at all times.

With the use of a rug frame you can concentrate fully on your hooking, without struggling to hold the pattern in place at the same time as you work. Take your pick from the following frames:

1. *Easel frame* (fig. 1). The easel frame is a wooden frame measuring about 18 x 36 inches, set onto a wooden or steel standard, with or without a foot rest. Its position is adjustable, and it is self-supporting, which eliminates the inconvenience of using a table for its support. When not in use, it may be folded together easily by loosening the frame in the slots and allowing it to hang vertically. *The easel frame is the most popular frame for all kinds of hooking* and is available at nearly all art needlework departments. For making your own easel frame, see fig. 2.

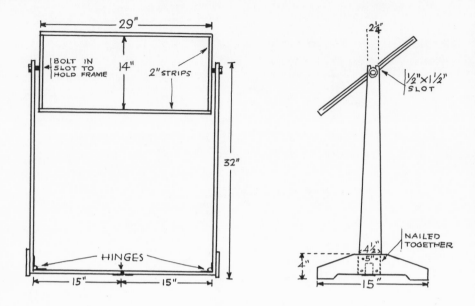

Fig. 2. Homemade easel frame, front and side view. Note hinges at bottom so that when frame at top is removed standard folds for convenient storing.

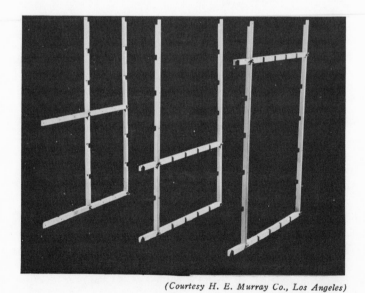

(Courtesy H. E. Murray Co., Los Angeles)

Fig. 3. Adjustable frame. This model can be adjusted to openings from 6 to 36 inches square.

2. *Adjustable frame* (fig. 3). The adjustable frame consists of four strips of wood, with slots for adjusting its size from as little as 6 inches square, to an in-between size, or even as large as 36 inches square. The adjustable frame is also available at many art needlework departments, and can be had at a very nominal cost.

3. *Small homemade frame* (fig. 4). This handy frame can be quickly assembled from four strips of wood. The thickness of each piece should be about 1 inch square, or a little more or less, according to what wood may be readily available. The length of your wood strips will be deter-

3 NAILS

Fig. 4. Homemade frame which can easily be constructed from four pieces of soft wood, two of them 18 inches long, the other two 24 inches long for a convenient working size.

mined by the size of the frame you desire. Use softwood or pine for easier use of thumbtacks. Strips are screwed or nailed together at ends to form a hollow rectangular square. Screws at the corners will make a sturdier frame, and steel brackets fastened to the inside corners will give further strength, though these are not essential. A very practical size for the frame is 18 by 24 inches. The writer has found this size and type of frame practical enough to make dozens of rugs, from small to room size. For both the homemade and the adjustable frame you will need a table against which it can be leaned while working. These simplest of frames are popular for their convenience in carrying to a class or to other group meetings common among rug hookers everywhere.

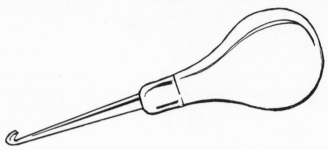

Fig. 5. Short wooden-handle hook.

HOOK NEEDLES (RUG HOOKS)

There are two types of hook needles or rug hooks. (Three, if we count the variation of the short wooden-handle hook with the curved shank steel hook.) These are:

1. *Short wooden-handle hook* (fig. 5). This standard type hook (used for hooking cut strips of material) consists of a crochet hook, or other such straight steel hook, set into a short wooden handle. Its size varies from fine to coarse, as does the length of the handle. While varying lengths and sizes are widely used, a medium-fine hook with a short wooden handle is recommended, with an overall length of about 4½ inches. The short handle enables one to hold the hook with the end of the handle resting against the palm of the hand, thus operating with a stronger grasp. However, if you are more comfortable holding your hook as you would a pencil, that is permissible, but try the other position first, as it seems to strengthen the hand movement.

Should it be inconvenient to obtain the short wooden-handle hook, you can make one by cutting (or filing) in two the shank of a steel crochet hook of a medium size. Make the length about 2 inches and insert the cut end into a wooden handle with a rounded top. The overall length should be about 4½ inches. By prying the steel hook into the wooden handle, it is surprising how quickly and firmly it is assembled. This is usually a job for the man of the house.

If you are obliged to purchase a hook with a longer handle than is recommended, it can easily be cut down to a shorter length. Always finish by rounding its edge.

The ideal hook is one fine enough to do good work, and which is comfortable to handle. It costs fifty cents to a dollar, and should improve with age if you take care of it.

2. *Short wooden-handle hook, with curved shank steel hook.* This hook is like the one just described except for its curved shank. Though it is often used, it isn't as popular as the straight hook. It is also available at art or needlework counters for less than one dollar. The results from both the above hooks are the same, and you will only discover your preference by trying them both out.

3. *Hollow-handle hook needle* (fig. 8). This type of hook is required for making rugs in yarn, or punch-work rugs as they are often called. The hook has a special handle, incorporating yarn guide and lock, and the self-threading tubes provide a needle for different kinds and weights of yarn. It sells at art needlework counters for less than two dollars.

MATERIALS FOR HOOKING RUGS

Materials for hooking rugs may be yarns made for that purpose, or from various woolen materials cut into strips. The two cannot be mixed, the choice of one or the other type of rug must be made at the start and the proper needle acquired. Yarn rugs are more expensive to make, but, as stated before, are worked more quickly than the other type. Another advantage with yarn rugs is that correct colors are assembled without difficulty when specifically purchased, while with woolen materials some effort may be required to collect suitable shades. In the end, however, the rug made with cut strips is not only of trifling cost by comparison, but is more practical for hard wear. Also, its body is of sufficient texture to require no special backing or lining, as is recommended for the yarn rug. There is no comparison, from the author's point of view, between a yarn rug and the beauty of one hooked with cut strips, the latter possessing more character and charm, but there are many who may not agree on this point.

Only 100 per cent woolen material should be used for hooking rugs—because of its greater wearability and soil resistance. This point cannot be overemphasized. Suitable hooking material for cutting into strips is likely to be found among the following old woolens: skirts, trousers, bathrobes, slacks, baby clothes, coats, overcoats, scarves, shawls, socks, bathing suits, mackinaws, and certain closely knit sweaters. Band and army uniforms may also be used to good advantage, and so can old blankets of various sizes.

Smooth and close weaves make the best hooking materials, with flannels heading the list. Broadcloth, jersey, suede, and blanket materials are also excellent for all around use. Materials with limited use are: tweeds, serges, sweaters, bathing suits, checks, plaids, gabardines, and highly colored woolens such as scarlet, kelly green, orange. Tweeds are excellent for a homespun effect in a hit-or-miss pattern or in certain borders and backgrounds; serges are only suitable when the material doesn't pull apart; checks and plaids are often good for the center of flowers, for veining of scrolls and leaves, for backgrounds if the colors are neutral; gabardines work best in a good heavy grade. Bright colors in small amounts are often useful for highlights in certain patterns and in hooked wall pictures, but are overpowering in large quantities in the average rug.

Materials not recommended are coarse tweeds and other open-weave fabrics, thin serges, any materials which are weak or rotten, woolens with other material mixed in such as rayons, cottons, etc.

Whenever possible, I suggest that the beginner use only smooth flannel until the technique of hooking is thoroughly mastered, as this is the easiest material to work with. After really acquiring the hooking knack, ruggers often use many materials which a beginner would find hard or even impossible to work with. So much depends on knowing how to handle the material as one hooks.

Moth-eaten woolens. These are the most popular hooking materials of all, for we all feel perfectly justified in cutting them into strips to go into a rug.

All hooking material should have seams ripped apart, and be washed thoroughly before being worked up into a rug. Garments that are dry-cleaned still need to be washed before hooking, because the washing will soften the material, and make it more pliable. The shrinking of the woolen improves its hooking texture because the weave is thickened.

Checking for a cotton thread. Avoid woolens with a cotton thread, as found, for instance, in some white flannels. Though the occasional thread may not prevent good wear, it will usually show to disadvantage after being hooked, especially as it does not dye the same color as wool. Test for cotton by breaking the thread in question. A cotton thread breaks sharply, while the woolen thread unwillingly pulls apart, leaving a ragged fuzzy end.

Color to collect. For specific patterns, naturally the exact colors planned are the ones to seek out first in existing materials, but for general collection white is the first color to assemble in quantity, for it may be dyed any color you want with the greatest ease. Next are the pastels, which can also be dyed quite readily when required. Tans and beiges are generally useful for backgrounds. Many other shades of medium and dark can also be worked into the average rug pattern without dyeing. Plaids, tweeds, and checks are fine for unusual touches, and give a rug character. Never turn down any offer of woolen material even if the shades seem unlikely to be useful, for dark colors can be bleached lighter and bright colors can be toned down by tinting.

SOURCES FOR OBTAINING WOOLENS

The family's discarded woolens are the first source of supply, as well as those of relatives and friends, if you can persuade them to send theirs your way. Rummage sales are perhaps the hooker's best friend, with thrift shops and salvage stores, such as the Goodwill and Salvation Army stores running a close second. Mill end stores and remnant sales can produce excellent material too. Some specialty stores make a business of catering to hookers by selling new pieces of woolens in various colors by the pound. If your sources are limited, one yard of new white woolen flannel, of 54-inch width, is sufficient, when dyed, to hook the flowers and leaves in a 3 by 5 foot rug. The value of your finished rug will more than compensate for any such occasional investment. Fortunately backgrounds of beiges and tans, and dark colors for borders as well, are usually acquired with little or no effort.

MISCELLANEOUS EQUIPMENT

Scissors (and cutters). Sharp scissors are a necessary part of your equipment. Among other uses, they are satisfactory for cutting rug strips, though for this purpose there are also many fine commercial cutters available. These will cut several strips at a time, and with finer results. While commercial cutters are certainly not imperative to beautiful rugs, they do save much time, especially for backgrounds, and if you plan to do many rugs you may find them a good investment. For companies selling these cutters, see advertisements in needlework magazines. Curved shears are convenient for certain trimming, though not essential.

Thumbtacks and staples. Whichever type of frame you use, ordinary thumbtacks are necessary to attach your pattern securely to the frame. As your rug progresses and becomes heavier, you will find yourself needing extra long thumbtacks or small staples.

Carpet binding. If carpet binding is sewed on the edge of the border before it is hooked, you will find it much more convenient when you come to hem it. Not only does carpet binding give the rug a neater appearance, but it adds to its wearing quality. Be sure to use only carpet binding that is made to be sewed on, not the binding that is chemically treated to be applied with a hot iron.

Whisk broom or brush. A whisk broom is useful to keep your work presentable, as you can't tell how your work looks if you don't keep it brushed.

Hammer, screw driver, nails, and screws. If you are putting together your own frame you will need a hammer and nails, or if you use screws for a firmer construction then you will need four screws and a screw driver. Holes must first be bored in the ends of the strips of wood to get the screws started. You will also need a hammer to drive in the staples that hold the burlap to the frame. Keep the screw driver handy for removing staples and thumbtacks.

3
PREPARING THE BURLAP

For hooking either with yarns or with strips of material, the preparation of the burlap or pattern is much the same. Before any hooking begins, the very first step is to hem the pattern's edge, preferably by machine, to prevent fraying (unless this has already been done on a bought pattern). Turn about ¼ inch of the edge to the back in one fold, and sew or machine-stitch along the edge of fold with strong cotton thread. After the pattern is thus hemmed, there should be a remaining space of at least 1½ inches between the border line of the pattern and the outside edge of the burlap. You will then be saved the inconvenience of working too close to the frame.

SEWING RUG BINDING ON PATTERN (fig. 7)

Before starting to hook, one edge of the rug binding should be sewed along the edge of the pattern so that when the rug is hooked the binding can be turned over the edge of the canvas and basted along its unsewed edge on the underside of the rug with long blind stitches. Do not miter corners as these are taken care of when hemmed. If no binding is used, allow for a 2-inch hem instead. A binding, however, makes a neater looking job at the edge of the finished rug. Use a binding that matches the color of the rug's border if possible. A white binding tape could be dyed, otherwise use a neutral shade such as beige or tan with a light border, or brown or black with a dark one.

(Photo: George de Gennaro)

Fig. 6. Attaching pattern to frame with thumbtacks. Note short-handle hook for hooking cut strips of material.

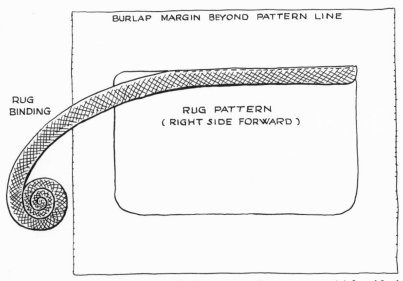

BURLAP MARGIN BEYOND PATTERN LINE

RUG BINDING

RUG PATTERN
(RIGHT SIDE FORWARD)

Fig. 7. Rug binding tape is sewed along edge of rug pattern (right side forward) in one strip before hooking begins. When hooking is finished excess burlap is cut off to within a half inch of binding and tape is folded over raw edge and basted on underside for a neat edge. To demonstrate the above clearly, the drawing shows a wider margin of burlap than would normally be left around the pattern.

On *punchwork rugs*—those done with yarn using a hollow-handle hook —you must establish the edge of the pattern on the reverse side of the rug, since this will be the right side when finished. Sew the binding along the edge on the opposite side to the pattern, so that this can be turned over the edge of the burlap as described above and basted on the underside of the rug—the side that faces you while punching the yarn through the burlap pattern.

ATTACHING PATTERN TO FRAME (fig. 6)

If you are using the easel type of frame, first set this up. Then, on whatever frame you are using, the same instructions apply. There are two methods of attaching the pattern to the frame.

1. *With thumbtacks or carpet tacks.* First of all double the material in a small fold of about ½ inch along the edge where the thumbtacks are to be used. This will prevent the threads of the burlap from pulling apart. Now stretch the rug pattern from opposite points as you thumbtack the edges to the frame. Starting at one corner, stretch the pattern tight down one side, and thumbtack the second corner. Fill in with thumbtacks down the same side, spaced at about 2-inch intervals. Then stretch the canvas tight as you thumbtack the third and fourth corners. Fill in with thumb-tacks, so the canvas is evenly secured and quite taut. Small carpet tacks may be substituted for thumbtacks, if preferred.

2. *The pattern may be attached to the frame by sewing* back and forth between the pattern and the frame with strong thread or twine. In this case no tacks are needed. Be sure to fold burlap so the thread goes through a double thickness, otherwise there will be too much pull at the edges of the burlap. Where the pattern is too narrow to reach across a large frame, it will be necessary to sew back and forth across a larger area, as shown in fig. 1. If you wish to avoid this, you can stitch a strip of any kind of strong material to the edge of the pattern so it will reach across the full width of the frame. If another piece is sewed on in this manner, just thumbtack down the edge, keeping the rug pattern tautly stretched.

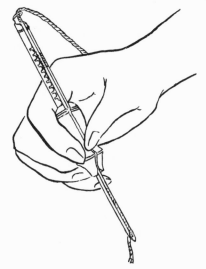

Fig. 8. Hollow-handle hook for hooking with yarn. Loops are hooked by plunging needle as far as possible through underside of canvas or warp cloth.

4

HOW TO HOOK WITH YARNS, USING HOLLOW-HANDLE HOOK

After hemming and fixing the burlap pattern to the frame as described in the previous chapter and assembling the bought yarn in the colors required for the design, you are ready to start hooking.

HOOKING

With lightweight yarn, thread your needle, according to manufacturer's instructions, and practice working outside the pattern first, then start working in the lower right-hand corner. Plunge the needle through the burlap, hold yarn, and on the reverse side pull end of yarn through (fig. 9). Always hold needle in vertical position. Never lift needle right above burlap (fig. 10), but bring point just to the surface and over 2 threads of burlap, plunging needle in as far as possible to make each stitch. Continue across rug from right to left, making a straight row of loops. On the last stitch of the row, cut yarn halfway up the needle on underside (fig. 11). Make sure the yarn feeds freely over the back of the hand and through the needle. Otherwise uneven loops or none at all will result.

As you are hooking, with the tips of your fingers always hold the loops of a finished row toward you underneath the burlap. This is possible because loops are high on the underneath side, which will be the top of the rug when finished. This keeps your work even, and the loops from mixing, making it easier to cut later. (Fig. 12.)

Hooking with yarn, using the hollow handle hook.

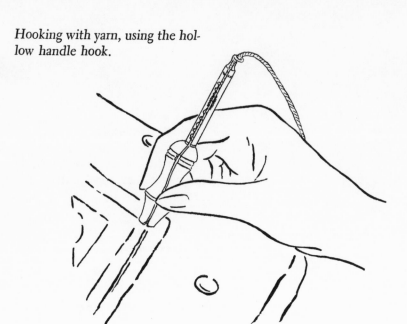

Fig. 9. Hooking a loop at the corner of the pattern (right side down).

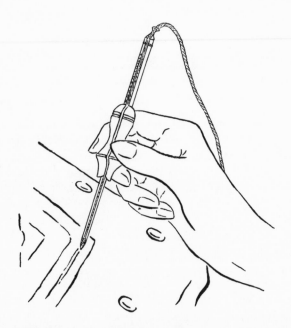

Fig. 10. Never lift the needle right above the pattern. The point is brought just to surface and over two threads, is then plunged down again for next loop.

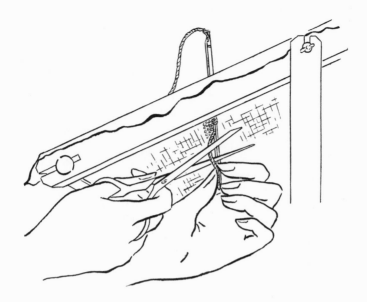

Fig. 11. Hooking proceeds in even rows from right to left. On last stitch of row, cut yarn halfway up needle on underside.

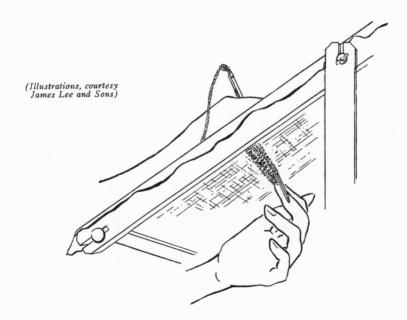

Fig. 12. With the left hand hold loops of finished row towards you underneath with tips of fingers. This keeps work even, the loops from meshing.

When working next to the seam of the rug binding or the border line of the pattern, hook 2 rows parallel to this line, hooking in every hole of the burlap mesh. This makes a firm edge right around the rug.

For the balance of the background, *skip 2 threads* of burlap mesh for each stitch on the first line, continuing across the pattern from right to left to make a row. Work a second row above the first but *with 1 cross thread* of mesh between the rows. For the third row *skip 2 cross threads* above the second row, since you will find the tension of the burlap becoming tighter—and continue as for the first row. Thus the background is continued alternating these three rows. Work the background to within 1 stitch of the central design and cut yarn. Continue hooking always from right to left, and in the one line space thus left along the outside of design, work one row of *background* color around, following the line of design (fig. 14). Next work one row of the *design* color forming an outline on right-hand side only, for filling in. Continue working design from right

(Illustrations, courtesy James Lee and Sons)

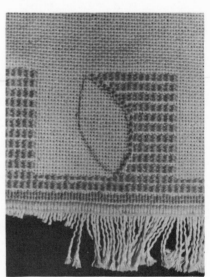

Fig. 13.   Fig. 14.

Fig. 13. Border lines of the pattern do not always follow weave of warp cloth. Follow lines of design, skipping rows when necessary. Each row is hooked with one cross thread of cloth between.

Fig. 14. Work background colors to within a stitch of design on each row, then outline design in background color, following line of design as shown.

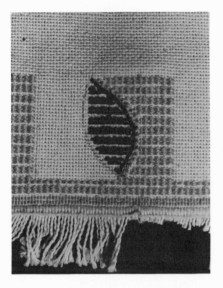

Fig. 15.   Fig. 16.

Fig. 15. Next to outline in background color, work outline in color of the design itself and fill in area as shown, hooking from right to left. Never work above or beyond any finished area.

Fig. 16. The same detail is outlined on the opposite side and hooking in rows is resumed.

Fig. 17. Oriental design hooked in yarn with the hollow-handle hook

to left, until filled in. Then finish by outlining design on the left side to complete outline already hooked on the right side. Never work above or beyond any unfinished space (figs. 15 and 16).

The entire rug is hooked in straight lines, in the burlap mesh, except for the outlines, which follow the design. Doing only a part of this outlining at a time will keep the loops from meshing, and thus form a clearer pattern.

FINISHING THE RUG

Loops should be cut and trimmed with the rug off the frame. When one area has been finished within the space of the frame, and before attaching the rug again to the frame for the next section to be hooked, fold the finished work over the left hand so the loops will stand up for easier cutting. Pick up loops with the scissors blade and cut through the center (fig. 18). After loops are cut, trim lightly for an even pile.

BEVELING (fig. 19)

Any or all of the design may be beveled, which means that this part will be raised from the background of the rug. Beveled sections are hooked in the same manner as previously described, except that the needle must be set in *slot 4* for the raised part of the design, working *every row* with one thread between rows. Cut loops as before with sharp-pointed scissors and mold the edges to form the beveling as desired.

(Courtesy James Lee and Sons)

Fig. 18. Yarn loops can be cut and trimmed as work progresses, but it is better to do this off the frame as shown. Cut loops through center with scissors, then trim lightly to an even pile.

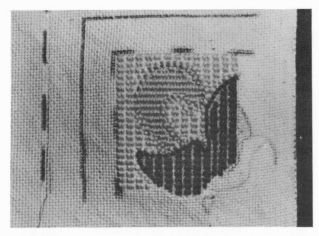

Fig. 19. Any or all of a design may be beveled. Such raised portions of the rug are worked the same way but the needle must be set in slot 4 for the raised part, working every row with one thread between rows. Cut loop in usual manner and mold edges to form beveling.

HEMMING THE RUG

When the rug has been hooked, cut off any excess burlap to within ½ inch of the binding seam, so the edges will be out of sight when the binding is sewed back. Press binding back lightly with warm iron before sewing, so it will lie perfectly flat and smooth during this operation. Use strong thread of matching or suitable neutral shade in either light or dark, depending on the border color. Taking care to fold the corners at neat right angles, sew long blind stitches, securely fastening the tape's edges. Any other fullness in binding may be equalized in tiny pleats, permitting the binding to lie smoothly along the bottom edge of the rug.

SIZING THE YARN RUG

While patterns of warp cloth do not need sizing because of the heavy texture, patterns on burlap do require it. Sizing prevents the burlap from kicking up at the corners, and encourages the whole rug to lie perfectly flat. Suitable sizing material is sold in art stores, and each brand comes with its own special directions.

When using sizing, place the finished rug upside down on the floor or on a table. Be sure it has been shaken out well and is clean. Then, with a clean paintbrush, apply the sizing over the burlap until the material has been completely covered. Let it dry thoroughly before placing the rug on the floor.

(Courtesy Callaway Mills, New York)

Two rugs hooked with yarn. Above: poinsettia design with bevel (raised) border. The color scheme is red for the flowers with green leaves on a gray background. Below: wedding ring motif in low-relief beveling, all one color.

Diamond Plaid. Hooked cotton rug of high, luxurious cut pile.

The multicolored rug in the foreground, called *The Broken Wreath*, was copied by the author from a museum pattern. Both this and the one in the dining room beyond are hooked from cut strips of material with a short-handle hook. Note also hooked pedals of the organ; chair coverings are in needlepoint.

(Photo: Lindburg Studio)

5

HOW TO HOOK WITH CUT STRIPS, USING A SHORT-HANDLE HOOK

CUTTING THE STRIPS FOR HOOKING

Strips should always be cut on the straight of the material, and never on the bias. Otherwise they may pull apart as they are being hooked. If uncertain of straight edge, tear material first, so you have a true straight line to follow. Cut strips about ⅛ inch wide for flowers and leaves, and slightly wider for other detail and background. A good rule to follow is to cut as finely as possible for floral details, as this permits more shading to be used. But do not cut so fine that strips pull apart when hooked. In planning your material, bear in mind that thin flannels may require slightly wider cutting than that of heavier woolens. Also woolen jerseys need wider cutting since they pull thinner when hooked. For the same reason, strips made from jerseys need to be hooked slightly higher. Cut strips may be of any length, but a 12- to 15-inch strip is a good average for general use.

HOW TO HOOK WITH CUT STRIPS

To begin hooking, hold the end of a cut strip in the left hand underneath the pattern at the place where you wish to start hooking. Don't fold the strip as its width (⅛ inch) has been correctly cut for good work. (Only when working with very thin material should you cut it double width and fold in half.) Hold your hook in the right hand with end of handle resting

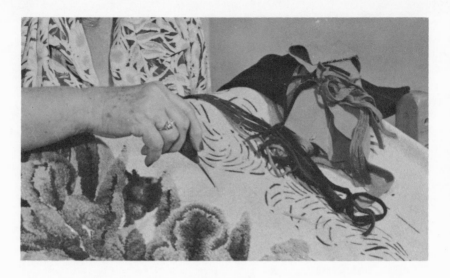

Fig. 20. Working with a short-handle hook. Note cut strips at right and additional material handy for cutting as these colors are needed.

against palm of hand, or if left handed, reverse your hand positions. Make sure that the side point of hook is to the left, with its smooth side to the right as you look down at the hook (fig. 21).

Push the hook through the burlap, and far enough down for the hook to grasp one end of the cut strip you are holding in your left hand (fig. 22). Continue holding the rest of the strip as you pull the hook back up with the first end through the burlap mesh. Pull the strip up until its end stands about ½ inch up from the burlap. Next, with the hook released, plunge it into the adjoining space in the burlap mesh, which means skipping one thread, and this time catch a *loop* of the same strip near where your left hand is holding the material. Pull this loop up through the burlap to a height of about ¼ inch, or slightly higher if you prefer. You now have one end standing ½ inch high and one loop standing ¼ inch high. Continue to pull loops up this way, through different spaces, until you reach the end of the strip. Be sure to pull loops high enough to stay hooked (fig. 23).

The difficulty many beginners have in hooking is caused by the fact they don't push the hook through the burlap far enough to conveniently grasp the loops for pulling through. If your first loop pulls out before the second is hooked, you are only experiencing what most hookers go through while learning. Try again, and this time pull slightly higher, to make allowances for it being pulled back when the following loop is pulled through. A slight twist of the wrist regulates the height of the loops as

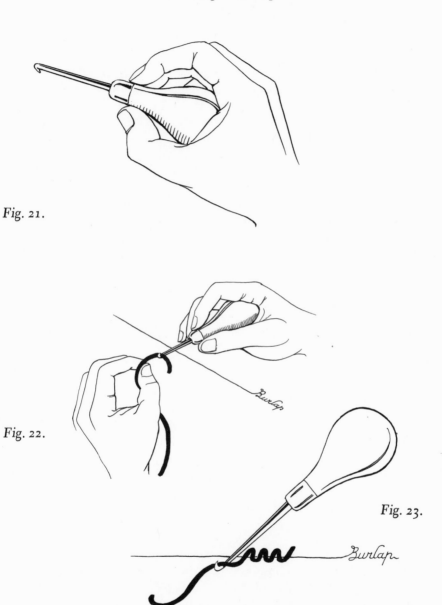

Fig. 21.

Fig. 22.

Fig. 23.

Fig. 21. The correct position for holding the hook—seen from above.
Fig. 22. Guiding the cut strip onto the hook after plunging the latter *through canvas.*
Fig. 23. Cross-sectional view showing how loops look while working with a cut strip. Be sure to pull loops high enough to hold their position.

each one is released. Keep practicing, and make sure that the strip to be hooked is kept untwisted and straight as you hook each loop.

SKIPPING SPACES

Continue hooking loops in the manner described, skipping a space or a double thread in the weave of burlap about every third or fourth loop. You will need to do this to prevent the loops from being overcrowded. *There is no set rule on the space skipping.* When your loops begin to crowd, always skip a space or double thread. When you reach the end of the strip, pull the end through to the right side of the pattern, and clip it even with the loops. The end you first pulled through should now also be clipped even. No sewing or fastening of the loops or ends is necessary since the weave of the burlap tightens more and more as each loop is added, and after some hooking is done, the loops are securely locked in. The next strip is hooked in the same manner.

MAKING UNIFORM LOOPS

Practice making loops as near the same height as possible, but don't let it worry you if there is some variation. It will take a certain amount of time to develop evenness in hooking. It is often a good idea for the beginner to practice hooking on the burlap outside the pattern first. Also, when actually starting on the rug pattern, it is best to begin by hooking a straight row along the border edge. The technique of uniform loops is thus somewhat mastered before more difficult hooking is attempted, such as on a flower design. It is always a simple matter to remove any loops that don't suit you by pulling the strip from underneath the pattern and starting again from the last loop with which you are satisfied. As already stated, practice will improve your hooking, so don't expect your best work when first starting out.

THE DIRECTION TO HOOK, AND HOW TO KEEP WORK EVEN

Always hook from right to left, unless you are left handed, in which case you will find it easier to hook in the opposite direction. After hooking each strip, check the reverse side of pattern to see if spaces look evenly filled. Large gaps or spacings between hooking are called windows, and these should be avoided as much as possible. Since we do not necessarily hook in straight rows as when hooking with yarns (chapter 4), we are more apt to have large vacant spaces in between our hooking unless we are careful. So always keep checking the reverse side as the work progresses to:
1. Avoid windows.
2. See that the hooking is smooth and with no bumps resulting from crossing one stitch over another as the loops are pulled through.

3. Avoid any looseness of the hooked strip between the loops. If you find this has happened, remove as many loops as necessary and replace the work in a more orderly manner.

HOW TO TURN WHEN HOOKING

When making a short turn, such as to reverse your hooking and go in an opposite direction, or even a right-angle turn, it is usually advisable

Fig. 24. Cutting a woolen strip for hooking. Note convenient way to keep hook between work.

Fig. 25. Comfortable way to hold small frame over edge of table while hooking.

to cut the strip on the top side and start again in the turned direction, rather than have the strip double over hooked work on the underside of the burlap or canvas.

DO NOT CLIP MORE LOOPS THAN YOU HAVE TO

Do not clip the tops of the loops any more than necessary, as unclipped loops wear better. Some clipping in the detail of the design is occasionally desirable to effect a closer blending of shading. It is also permissible to clip an occasional loop that you may find is standing higher than the rest—for a uniform look to your work is very important.

6

AN EASY PATTERN FOR THE BEGINNER TO MAKE

The easiest pattern to hook, and one anyone can sketch out in a couple of hours, is the block pattern. See fig. 26. It is also popular among beginners because it may be done with any woolens that are on hand. The results are both practical and effective.

Use a piece of ordinary burlap—even a clean burlap feed bag is usable. The size of the burlap should be slightly larger than 24 by 36 inches, so that an oblong square of that size may be marked off with at least a 2-inch margin all around. You will need this margin for attaching the pattern to the frame, as described in chapter 3.

MARKING OFF A 24-BY-36-INCH MEASUREMENT

First pull a thread from each end of the burlap. This will ensure that you have straight edges as a guide for ruling up your square. Next, spread the burlap out flat and with a ruler mark your 24 by 36 outside measurement centrally on the burlap, using black grease-chalk, or charcoal. Establish the corner points first, equalizing their distances from each edge, then draw in the connecting lines. Working this way you will find it easier to be accurate. Ideally, the corners of the burlap should be tacked on to a flat board during this and the next process.

Fig. 26. A floral block pattern. Note same design reversed in alternate blocks.

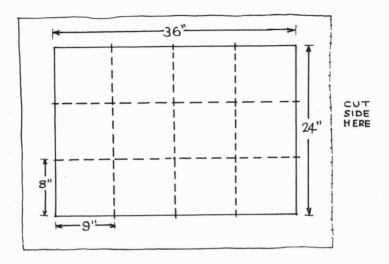

Fig. 27. How to mark off burlap for block pattern illustrated in fig. 26. The pattern measures 36 by 24 inches, the burlap 36 by 48 inches. Each block measures 8 by 9 inches. Surplus edge is trimmed off later.

MARKING OFF THE SQUARES FOR THE PATTERN

Using a ruler, divide one 24-inch end of the pattern into lengths of 8 inches. Mark 8-inch divisions (there will be two lines equally spaced between each side) at the other end of the pattern, then connect these marks with rules through the entire length of pattern area as shown in fig. 27.

Now follow the same procedure with the side, or wider edge, of the pattern area. Divide its width into 4 lengths of 9 inches, establishing divisional points on each side, then marking the connecting lines through the width of the pattern. This means you will draw three lines equidistantly between the outer lines of the pattern. You will now have completed the first step in making the block pattern illustrated, with a total of 12 squares, each measuring 8 by 9 inches.

PLAIN BLOCK VARIATIONS

This pattern can be designed to have one row less, making it a square of nine separate areas, or it can have as many more rows of squares as you wish for a larger rug. The method of marking remains the same whatever size you plan. Each square can be filled with a floral motif, as illustrated in fig. 26 and described next, or it can be plain for a more modern setting. If you plan to use plain colors, why not try a design with nine equal squares, alternating two colors in checkerboard fashion. Supposing you have chosen a color scheme of light and dark green or brown, or black and gray, or any

Fig. 28. Actual size spray suggested for an 8-by-9-inch block. Place centrally in each square, reversing design in alternate block as shown in fig. 26. You can use same tracing (on vellum paper) by going over lines first on one side of paper, then on the reverse side to make the flower face in different directions. Use carbon paper between the vellum and burlap.

other two shades of the same color, alternate your dark and light squares so you have:

Top row: dark   light   dark
Second row: light   dark   light
Third row: dark   light   dark

and so on. The checkerboard pattern looks better when it is worked out so that the squares in each corner are the same color, so watch out how many rows you plan. Other interesting checkerboard color schemes might be royal blue and chartreuse, pink and mauve, light blue and coral, or other combinations suited to the room for which the rug is intended.

DRAWING A SINGLE FLORAL SPRAY IN EACH BLOCK

Returning to our 24 by 36 rug with 12 squares, a small open petal flower with a couple of leaves, as in our illustration, makes an attractive design for the center of each block in the pattern. Use this design or any other that is to your liking. If you wish to use the one illustrated, place a thin transparent paper, such as tissue or white vellum paper directly over the design represented in fig. 28 and trace the entire spray, then proceed as described next.

TRANSFERRING THE DESIGN TO BURLAP

If you are using tissue paper for tracing your original design it will be necessary to transfer this to heavier paper so that, in turn, the design may be transferred to burlap. If you are using vellum paper, you should find this heavy enough for tracing your design directly onto the burlap. The pattern is transferred onto burlap by tracing with carbon paper directly underneath the pattern, using a blunt pencil for tracing the outlines.

Apart from the use of vellum paper recommended for easy tracing and transfer to the burlap, any brown paper may be used for transferring the drawing, such as wrapping paper, a grocery bag (cut down the sides and flattened out as a single sheet), etc. Pin paper over block in a few places before slipping carbon underneath, so your design will not slip as it is being transferred. Before removing drawing, check underneath to make sure lines are clear. Redraw the lines where necessary. In this manner, repeat drawing in all the blocks.

INKING IN THE TRACING

Though it may be possible to work from the carbon-drawn lines, it is generally best to ink the design in over the tracing so it will remain permanent. Do this with an ordinary pen and regular writing ink, or an old fountain pen.

Fig. 29. The block pattern is hooked beginning in upper right-hand block. Hook flower, leaves, and stem first, then fill in background with straight lines of hooking. Alternate lines from horizontal to vertical in alternate blocks as shown. Choose a neutral shade for background.

46

VARYING THE SPRAY'S POSITION

The position of the flower is more graceful if it is placed diagonally in each block. You can make the design face the same way in each block, but I think you will agree it makes a much more interesting composition when reversed in alternating blocks as in the fig. 26. For instance, in one block it slants from the upper left-hand corner, while in the adjoining block it slants diagonally from the upper right-hand corner. Thus each block in a row is alternated. Note that the second row begins with the flower in reverse position to the one in the block directly over it.

Fig. 28 shows how a single tracing, exact size, can be used to fill each block. With carbon paper underneath, the vellum is turned over, first with one side up, then with the other, while the design is transferred to the burlap. By this method of tracing over both sides of the transparent sheet, the design is reversed in each neighboring block, and is also correctly placed in each block without guesswork. This transfer is very simple to do. Slight variations in the drawing will not be noticed in the finished work. In fact, it is just such slight variations (in hooking, too) that give hand-hooked rugs so much more character than machine-made ones.

HOOKING THE BLOCK DESIGN

See general instructions in chapter 5, also notes under fig. 29.

7

HOOKING A RUG FROM START TO FINISH WITH THE SHORT-HANDLE HOOK

The pattern's edge must be hemmed to prevent the burlap from fraying, as described in chapter 3. Also the rug binding should be sewed on first, if possible, though it may be done later—before hooking the border—if that is more convenient.

Always attach your pattern to a frame before attempting to hook. Use numerous thumbtacks and attach the pattern as described in chapter 3.

WHERE TO BEGIN HOOKING

If doing a block or geometric pattern, it is better to start at the upper right-hand corner, and work across the rug from right to left. In other words, begin on the upper right-hand block. By doing this, you will avoid reaching over the hooked part of the rug as it progresses. The unworked part of the burlap pattern should be rolled or folded out of the way for greater convenience while hooking the area within the frame. Excess burlap can sometimes be pinned directly to the side of the frame so it doesn't get in your way; safety pins are also excellent for pinning a longer piece in a tight hanging roll.

WHAT TO HOOK FIRST IN THE BLOCK PATTERN

If you are new at hooking, you should practice some background work in the block first—outlining each block in the row, for instance—before starting a flower or other curved detail in the pattern. After that, if doing a floral block, begin by outlining the flower, and completing the center before filling in the petals. The leaves should also be outlined first, before you fill in. With the floral detail in a block completed, next you must fill in the background. In block patterns, backgrounds may be done in straight lines, in which case it will be more interesting if they run horizontally in one block, vertically in the next, as shown in fig. 29. Repeat the process for each block, working from right to left across pattern. Note: It is better always to outline the floral pattern first within a block so that proper contours will be retained when working the background.

DESIGN OF FLORAL CENTER AND SCROLL

In beginning a rug with a typical floral center and scroll, such as in fig. 30, place the pattern on the frame so as to start hooking in the center of the floral grouping. In this way, you work away from the center as the rug progresses, and thus avoid later having to reach over any hooked part of the pattern. Complete flowers and leaves before filling in background among such detail. In the flowers, do the centers first, then outline petals in order to fill in. The first step in hooking flowers is to assemble shades in light, medium, and dark for each color flower. This will give highlights and shadows to your work. You will find the subject of hooking different types of flowers and leaves is covered in detail in the next chapter.

When you have finished the floral center, move the pattern on the frame so you can begin hooking the scroll. After the scroll within the frame setting is finished, complete the background between the scroll and the floral center. Then it will be unnecessary to come back later to do any more filling in.

THE BORDER

Do the border of the rug last. Hook one row directly along the border line or the binding seam of the tape. This row must, of course, be straight on a square or rectangular rug, curved on a circular or oval rug. There should be a loop in nearly every hole, all the way around.

While the remaining space of the border may be filled in with circular or straight rows, following the outline of the rug, you may prefer to break up such spaces with wavy lines. However, the beginner usually finds it easier to hook in rows. Before filling in the border, always outline the scroll after it is hooked, with one row of the border color to preserve con-

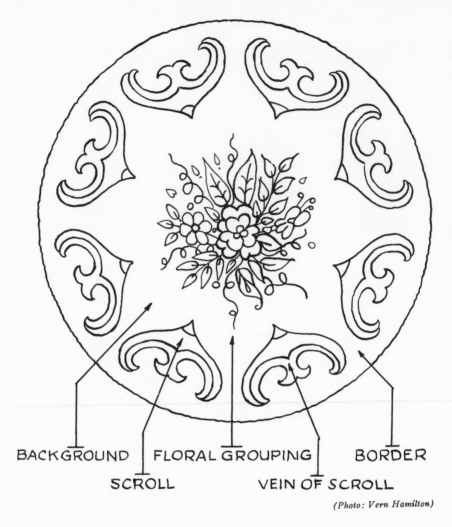

BACKGROUND | FLORAL GROUPING | BORDER

SCROLL | VEIN OF SCROLL

(Photo: Vern Hamilton)

Fig. 30. A typical traditional circular pattern.

tours. Detailed information about varied borders and scroll effects on rugs
will be found in chapters 16 and 18.

HEMMING THE RUG

The rug is hemmed as outlined in chapter 4.

PRESSING THE FINISHED RUG

A steam pressing is as necessary to the beauty of a rug as to a tailored
suit, and no hooked rug, made from strips of cut material, should be con-

(Photo: Vern Hamilton)

Lilies. A 32 by 54 inch oval rug designed and hooked by Beth Lucas.

This morning-glory rug was adapted from a quilt pattern by Nellie
Graves, who also hooked the rug. Note the modern scroll of leaf outlines.

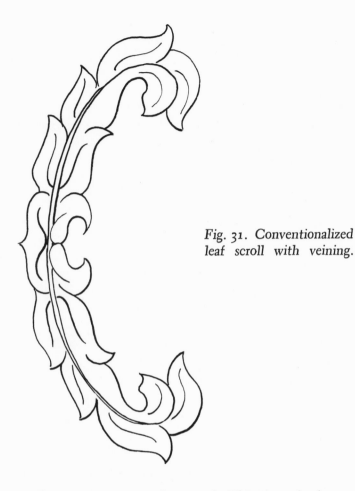

Fig. 31. Conventionalized leaf scroll with veining.

sidered finished until it is properly pressed. This not only shapes the rug so that it lies flat on the floor, but makes it desirably smooth and even. Pressing gives that important final professional touch to your workmanship.

It is done by placing the rug *upside down* on top of another *smooth* rug or padding. Next, wet a thin towel (not Turkish) or a part of an old sheet or cloth and squeeze out excess water. Spread the wet towel or sheet smoothly over the wrong side of the rug and, with a hot iron, press the entire surface. Take care always to have the wet toweling between the iron and the rug so that there is no chance of scorching the wool. Also make sure no part of the rug is left unpressed. Especially if using a small cloth, you will find it necessary to wet this as often as the iron dries it off. The hem line needs extra pressing to prevent any curling of edges or corners.

After the rug is pressed, turn right side up, and let dry overnight. It will then be ready for everyday wear. If given the ordinary care any good rug deserves, your masterpiece should last a lifetime—and more!

An oval rug with multicolored floral pattern in the collection of Mrs. Shirley Shunk.

8

SOURCES OF INSPIRATION FOR DESIGNS

While real flowers are the best inspiration for hookers, excellent ideas can also be gathered from innumerable other sources. As soon as possible every hooker should start a scrapbook with all kinds of floral illustrations which can be turned to for constant reference. Everyday we are likely to run across illustrations in magazines, papers, catalogs, advertisements, which, if saved, would greatly help us in our rug designs and shading.

Flower catalogs and seed packages. These are often very helpful to hookers who seek realism in their flowers and foliage. Take the pansy, for instance. This is clearly illustrated on a flower seed package, so that, even had you never seen one, you could still do a good job of duplication. The photograph or realistic illustration on the front shows the exact shape of the center, with its four different parts of three colors, as well as other pattern details. Equally worth while purchasing are seed packages of morning glories, phlox, sweet peas, poppies, petunias, marigolds, and others that take your special fancy as you see them displayed in a store. Flower catalogs also show beautiful illustrations of regal lillies, roses and rosebuds, jonquils, irises, and other blossoms appropriate to incorporate in a rug design. Many old-time ruggers always make it a practice to keep up to date with just such material each year.

WALL-PAPER BOOKS

If you are fortunate enough to acquire a wall-paper book, you may use it many times over for hooking ideas. By asking in advance, these books are often available at the end of the season. Every kind of a flower you can name (and many you can't) are included in these books. In one such collection, the writer found a priceless calla lily which worked out so beautifully in a rug design that everyone who sees it wishes to copy its exquisite coloring and detail. In classes, too, hookers have found wall-paper books worth their weight in gold, for when a new way of shading is desired they provide an almost endless source of inspiration.

Floral chintzes and other drapery material. Floral prints on fabrics provide wonderful lessons in color combinations, shading, and the general distribution of color in a design. Many hookers copy floral colors in draperies so that there will be a close relationship in the rug they are hooking to go in the same room.

Hand-painted china or pottery. Antique hand-painted china, or floral motifs on pottery are also worth studying. The writer has a favorite little bowl of Bavarian china that has yellow daisies shading into soft greens and light brown. Its coloring has been the inspiration for hooking many a daisy. Plates and platters with flowers or fruit also furnish many patterns. A lovely old china piece featuring luscious yellow-green grapes was traced, enlarged, and transferred to burlap for a most successful hooked rug. Another plate, with purple plums highlighted in pink, was re-created in a charming hooked chair seat. Such examples could go on indefinitely.

Greeting cards. The value of greeting cards also cannot be overemphasized. Have you wondered how to design and shade a band of ribbon, with its turns and twists? A greeting card showing this may provide just the right answer for a border design. Do you know how to shade a basket? Those natural tans and golden browns are perfectly illustrated on many a birthday card. Shells, bouquets of flowers, fruits, folk motifs, animals, winter scenes that can be hooked into a picture, and many other designs found on cards of all kinds are good source material for details and color. File those cards with the best shading ideas in your scrapbook, and retain others with lesser possibilities, for easy reference—just in case.

Decals. These are surprisingly good for shading ideas and are a pleasure to add to your growing scrapbook. Their colorings often have the richness of oil paintings and are clear and easy to follow.

Needlepoint. While needlepoint can't be included in the scrapbook, reproductions from magazines can. The study of good, original needlepoint is, of course, of inestimable help to the hooker, and reproductions in color come a close second. The yarn shadings are so clearly illustrated that hookers can copy the technique even to minute detail. As a matter of fact, you will find that you can often improve on needlepoint flowers when hooking in an assorted color series of finely cut strips of flannel. Smoother shadings can be obtained, and the curved rows that are possible in rug hooking are more graceful and less mechanical looking than the hard straight rows of needlepoint.

Detail of Dictionary pattern rug by K. Neal, made by Mrs. B. H. Sharp.

9

HOOKING FLOWERS AND LEAVES

The old-time method was to hook a flower or leaf from just one shade of color, outlining its contours in black. In this way no special shading was achieved. Charming though many of these primitive works are, there is no longer any necessity for us to limit ourselves, for materials are plentiful today and dyeing presents no problems at all. When desired, realism is easily achieved in a floral design by using *graduated shades* of any natural flower or leaf color. For easier reference, we will hereafter refer to such graduated shades—represented by different pieces of woolen material—as "color series."

COLOR SERIES

A color series may be three or more shades of a color accumulated from material on hand, as, for instance, light green, medium green, and dark green. Or a color series may consist of three or more shades of a color where the material has been dyed (see chapter 13). Color series should always be of blending tones. For example, blue-greens make one color series, while yellow-greens make another, therefore it is not consistent or successful to intermix the two different ranges in one color series.

Waldron Rose, copied from an old rug by Ellen C. Gould and hooked by Ruth Sattelkau.

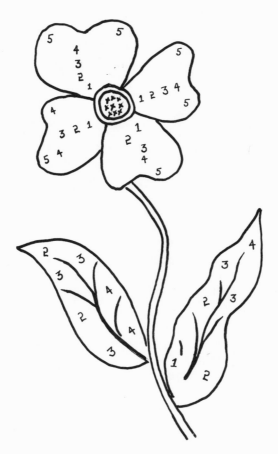

Fig. 32. Open-petal flower pattern. Color series marked represent: 1, light-est shade; 2, next to lightest shade; 3, medium shade; 4, next to dark; 5, darkest shade.

PURPOSE OF COLOR SERIES

In hooking natural flowers and leaves, it is as essential to feature their highlights as it is their shadowed areas—and the variety of shades assembled in a color series will enable you to do this. The in-between shades are used between the highlights and shadow lines to smooth out the shading. Obviously, the more shades you have in a color series, the smoother your shading can be. It is always desirable to have shades of more or less equal variation, so that your coloring in a flower will not suddenly jump from light into dark. Appropriate color series are planned in each case for the type of flowers included in your rug pattern. A large, importantly placed flower usually requires a larger color series than that of a smaller one.

OPEN-PETAL FLOWERS

These may be any one of a numerous variety of flowers such as the wild rose, dogwood, periwinkle, apple, cherry, or peach blossom, etc., in colorings of pink, blue, white, yellow, or other colors. This type of flower is usually considered the easiest of all to hook, with its small center surrounded by a few rather flat petals of simple outline as shown in fig. 32.

Centers are best hooked first, so they don't get squeezed out of shape when the petals are filled in. Plaid mixtures in bright greens, reds, yellows, browns, etc., can be most attractive in many of the open-petal flowers, often adding just the necessary touch. Plaids are particularly suited for oversize centers which some of these flowers feature. Or the flower with a double center might be worked in plaid, with a solid yellow surrounding it. The rim of a single center will require a row hooked with a strip cut from one of the dark colors in the plaid. This darker rim will emphasize depth, adding greatly to the natural molding of the flower. Mixtures such as those found in Paisley shawls and Scotch plaid skirts are especially suited for floral centers—as are brown-and-white shepherd checks, which can be tinted bright yellow. Other color suggestions for centers of open-petal flowers are as follows:

Pink flowers: ·yellow center, outlined with soft green.
Blue flowers: yellow-green center, outlined with yellow.
Yellow flowers: orange center, outlined with light green or brown.
White flowers: yellow center, outlined with bright orange.
Lavender flowers: yellow center, outlined with orange or yellow-green.

Petals of the open-petal flower may shade from an outline of light at the tip into dark next to the center of the flower, or vice versa. Always take into consideration the coloring of the background of the rug when outlining flowers or leaves, so as to make sure detail will not be lost when the work is completed. Dark backgrounds require light-tipped flowers, while a light background necessitates the use of more color at the edges of the petals. Thus, important details will show to good advantage.

In flower designs where one petal crosses over another, the overlapping petal should be outlined in a lighter shade than the lower petal. In this manner, when each has been filled in, proper emphasis will have been placed on the overlapping petal. By outlining petals first and then shading from light into dark, or vice versa, to complete each petal, good shading technique will be developed. For beginners it is best to finish one petal at a time before starting another, even though you may have outlined all the petals first to establish the pattern and general color scheme of the flower. Do not try to shade open-petal flowers in straight rows. It is always better to be guided by the outline of the petal. Where there is a pronounced curve in this outline, hook a short row for each full row

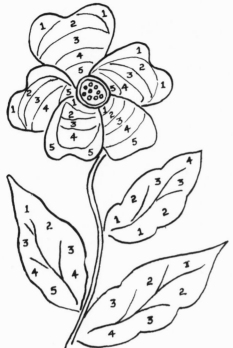

Fig. 33.

Variation of the open-petal flower pattern, shading from light to dark in the top three petals and from dark to light in the lower ones. Color series numbers 1 to 5 correspond to those given under fig. 32.

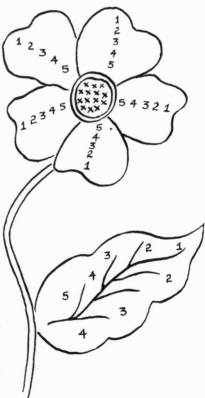

Fig. 34.

Another open-petal flower variation with lightest color at each petal edge. Color series 1 to 5 are the same as given under fig. 32.

around, as you continue to fill the petal in. The short rows need extend only across the outer part of the petal, stopping where the petal's edge sharply turns toward the center of the flower. Thus long and short rows may be used throughout the petal. Four or five shades in the color series is sufficient for the open-petal flower.

Leaves for this type of flower, like all others, should be outlined first, have the veins hooked next, and the background filled in afterwards.

CALLA LILY (fig. 35)

This flower needs about seven shades, plus two deep yellow shades for the stamen. The leaf takes five shades of green with a golden brown for the veining. Start the flower with the stamen, then work the graduated shades as listed under fig. 35. Next, follow the diagram for the leaves. Finish the stems to required length in light green.

Fig. 35. Calla lily pattern. A and b in the center of the flower represent bright yellow and deep yellow shades respectively. Colors 1 to 7 are as follows: 1, white; 2, creamy white; 3, light yellow; 4, light green; 5, light gray; 6, medium gray; 7, dark gray. Leaf color series is: 1, light green; 2, next to light green; 3, medium green; 4, next to dark green; 5, dark green. Veining of leaves is in golden brown.

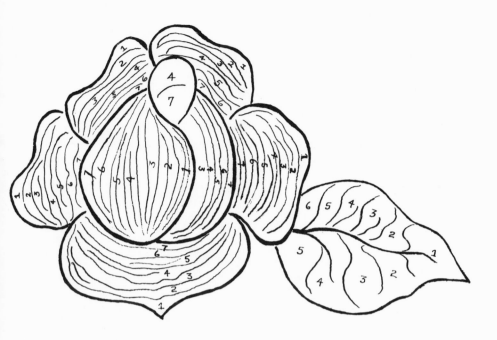

Fig. 36. Seven-shade rose pattern. Color series 1 to 7 is as follows: 1, lightest shade; 2, next to light; 3, medium light; 4, medium; 5, medium dark; 6, dark; 7, very dark. The leaf also grades from light to dark, 1 representing the lightest green. Leaf veins can be worked in rust-brown.

THE ROSE

This is the most popular flower motif of all. A minimum of four shades, and a maximum of seven or eight on a larger rose are needed to shade it attractively. One of the prettiest rose patterns is one showing a bud center framed with petals. (See fig. 36 and variation with fewer colors in fig. 37.)

1. Outline the petals in your lightest shade.
2. Do the outline around the center part of the rose (between petals and bud), using your darkest shade.
3. Hook the so-called question-mark line, using the lightest shade.
4. Fill in the heart of the rose with the three shades noted in the diagram, then the larger part of the bud. The trick of good shading in this area is to add one or more half lines for each of the longer lines hooked, using the same series of shades from light to dark. This will fill out the wider areas, allowing the full-length lines or

63

(*Photo: Vern Hamilton*)

Rose and Iris, designed by Kathleen Van Wyck and hooked by Kathryn Bill. The flowers are in subdued multifloral shades, the scroll is a harmonious green and the background light beige with a border of darker shades of the same color.

rows to follow the contour of the outline. Use more light than dark shades, for this is the very lightest part of the rose.

5. Fill in the smaller part of the bud. This is shaded in the same manner as the larger area. Note, however, that at its center edge you should start hooking with a darker shade than was used at the inner edge of the larger part. This color differential emphasizes the division of the two petals of the bud.

6. Shade the open petals from light at their outer edges into the medium shades, and finish with dark at the base of each of them. Again

Fig. 37. Four-shade rose pattern. Color series 1 to 4 represents light to dark, using color numbers 1, 3, 5, and 7 given under fig. 36. Leaf pattern also has reduced amount of green shading.

Fig. 38. Rosebuds. Shade from lightest rose color 1, to darkest 6, and hook leaves and stems in green, following same scheme as previous rose patterns.

it is best to hook occasional half or quarter rows to fill in between the full ones that follow the contour of the petal. In large petals add extra rows of the same shades in approximately equal amounts, as required. In small petals, you may find it necessary to eliminate one or more shades, but try not to change shades more abruptly than by skipping every other one. Sometimes, too, smaller petals are more effective by skipping the lightest shade, especially if they are on the outside, as at the top of the rose.

7. Rose leaves should next be hooked in bronze-green tones, veined with a rust color. This veining may be of a solid-colored material or a plaid mixture containing rust and brown tones.

Popular rose colors are: pink, red, or yellow. A color series from light to dark is easily assembled or dyed for any of these. White roses can be shaded with different colors as follows: white—very light beige, light green, soft pink, rose, and wine, or else try shades of beige and light through to dark gray.

Rosebuds (fig. 38) are shaded from the same materials used in series for the roses. Each petal is shaded to contrast with the adjoining one, and no two need be done quite alike. Highlights are essential, however, to give the necessary contrast in the small spaces.

The green parts of the bud should be hooked in light, medium, and dark bronze-green shades as used for the rose leaves. The light should be used in the center part with the darker tones next to the petal part of the rose.

The stems should be worked in greens which have been spot dyed with a bit of red to give a mottled effect. Some of the smaller leaves of the rose might also be made up in this coloring to form a pleasing variation.

A rose with a plaid center (fig. 39) is occasionally featured in a full-blown flower. Such a center can be effectively hooked with a mixture containing yellow, green, and orange, etc.—a tweed mixture of this coloring being especially suitable.

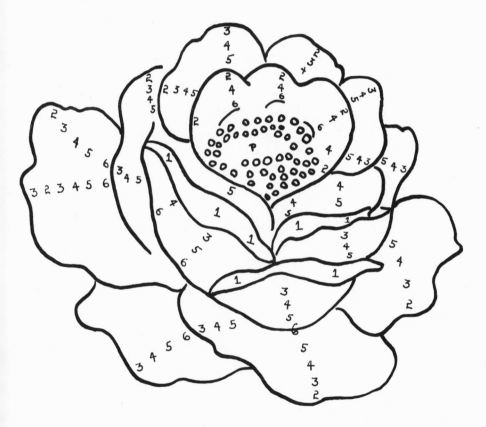

Fig. 39. Full-blown rose pattern. Hook in a color series of six shades of red from lightest 1 (pink) to darkest 6, as indicated. The circles in the center of the rose, and the center itself, marked P, are effective hooked in plaids containing yellow, orange, green, and possibly flecks of brown.

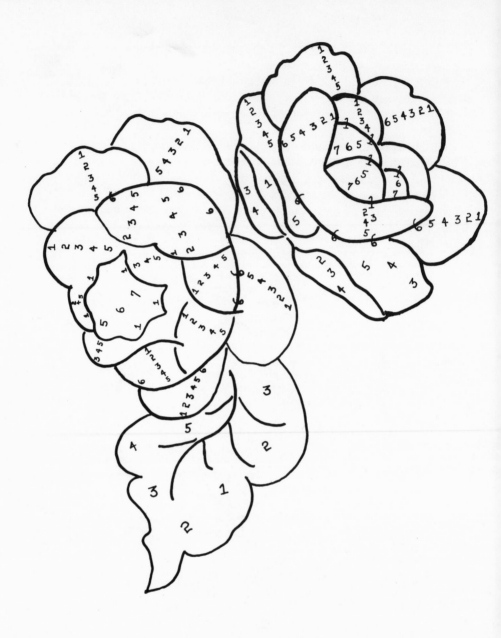

Fig. 40. White rose pattern. The color series is as follows: 1, pure white; 2, antique white; 3, light beige; 4, very light green; 5, very light pink; 6, shade darker pink; 7, garnet. The leaf is in light green (1) shading into dark (5).

JONQUILS (fig. 41)

These look lovely hooked in yellow tones shading into either golden-brown or rust tones. A touch of plaid, especially Scotch plaid, containing red, orange, and brown tones, is very pleasing when used in the center. Otherwise, the top of the center is kept in the lighter tones, while the bowl is made to contrast with the shades of each touching petal. Petals are shaded from light to dark as for other flowers.

Fig. 41. Jonquil pattern. Hook in shades of yellow and rust in the following manner: 1, light yellow; 2, medium yellow; 3, bright yellow; 4, yellow with a slight rust cast; 5, deeper yellowish rust; 6, shade deeper yellowish rust. The heavy line in the top center, marked P, can be hooked in contrasting plaid.

BLUEBELLS (fig. 42)

Bluebells need about six graduated shades of blue with a touch of green around a bright yellow center. The leaves require several shades in tones of jade green, veined with a medium shade of brown, or dark green.

DAISIES (fig. 43)

These may be made in either the white coloring used for the calla lily in fig. 35, or in shades of yellow or purple. The shades should be of graduated tones to emphasize the separate petals.

The center may be hooked in a bright contrasting plaid, or it might be a small brown check dyed a bright yellow. If necessary, outline the center with a dark row of a solid coloring to give emphasis. A white or purple daisy looks well with a dash of light green in the center, encircled by buttercup yellow, while a brown check is especially suitable for a yellow daisy.

Fig. 42. Bluebell pattern. The color series marked represents: 1, light blue; 2, shade darker; 3, medium blue; 4, medium dark blue; 5, dark blue; 6, very dark blue. Hook the center of the flower marked (a) in light yellow-green, (b) in buttercup yellow. Leaves are in green with dark veins. Stems are light brown.

Fig. 43. Daisies can be hooked in yellow, purple, or in white, yellow, green, and gray as used for the calla lily in fig. 35. As usual 1 represents the lightest shade and 6 the darkest. The center can be hooked in contrasting plaid or bright yellow mixture.

Leaves of daisies are hooked in the color green that looks best with the shade of the flower. A safe shade for any colored daisy would be a muted gray-green, since this is a good neutral tone. Otherwise you might try jade green with blue daisies, bronze green with yellow or pink flowers. The daisy leaf is rather wide and looks best with dark green or brown veining, whichever ties in best with the general color scheme of the rug.

TULIPS (fig. 44)

Tulips are usually hooked in yellow or purple shades. The colorings used for yellow daisies or purple grapes can be used if you are dyeing a series for either of these. Be sure to make the petals contrast with one another by using light on one petal where it touches the dark part of another.

Leaves for the tulips are made from five graduated shades of jade green, veined with either brown, chartreuse, or dark (forest) green. The stem should be two graduated shades of the dark green used in the leaf.

LEAVES

Leaves of the various flowers deserve their share of attention, as they emphasize the beauty of each blossom. Several shades of green in both cool and warm tones should be used for different leaves in a floral group-

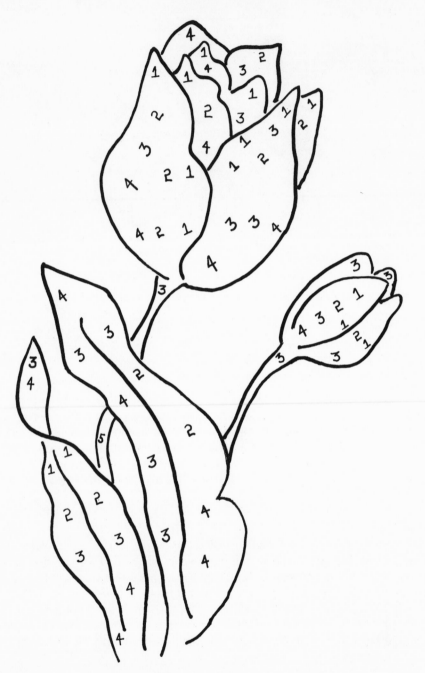

Fig. 44. Tulip pattern (golden yellow). Hook 1 in light gold, 2 in next to light gold, 3 in medium gold, 4 in dark golden brown. The flower can also be hooked in reds or other tulip colors. Leaves shade from light green (1) to dark (4).

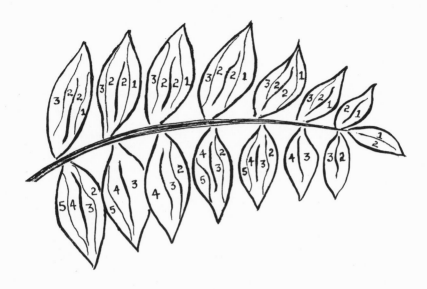

Fig. 45. Fern pattern. Use a green color series from lightest shade, 1, to darkest, 5. Stem and veins can be hooked in brown.

ing. As nearly as possible, accompany each flower with its natural leaf and foliage coloring. Rose leaves, for instance, call for bronze greens, while morning glories need medium bright green. Lavender flowers such as phlox should have gray-green leaves, while pansy leaves are best worked out in soft kelly tones.

Leaves are usually considered easier than flowers to shade. Be sure that the vein will afford a pleasing contrast to the leaf tones, and always complete this part first. Plaids are often used successfully for veining, and other general suggestions include: dark green, dark brown, golden brown, brown check, rust, cocoa, gold, chartreuse, and occasionally yellow or tan.

THE FERN (fig. 45)

This should have a series of bronze-green shades, with one side shaded lighter than the other for the most interesting effect. To dye these shades, use bright green over beige material, or add a bit of golden brown to bright green if dyeing over white material.

The center stem should be of a dark contrasting tone of golden brown or cocoa, and the same should be used for the short fine vein in the center of each leaf.

10

ADDITIONAL NOTES ON FLORAL AND LEAF SHADINGS

The examples of flowers and leaves so far given represent the technique of shading in layers. Other types of flowers and foliage call for a slightly different method of working—usually termed "fingering in."

FINGERING IN SHADES

Flowers, such as the morning glories, irises, pansies, poppies, and other blossoms with irregular streaks in their petals or foliage require that their shades be fingered in for realism. This really means to thread shades in as you go from one strip to the next, somewhat as you thread your fingers when you clasp your hands together. In this manner your shades interlace one another over all or part of the petal or leaf. The morning glory pattern in fig. 46 is a perfect example to take, since all of its shades, with the exception of its center and contour outline, are best fingered in as shown.

MORNING GLORY (fig. 46)

Note that shade 3, light blue, is used to outline the edge of the entire flower. The upper edge is made twice the width of the lower edge to give the flower perspective. The yellow center is next added, followed by the five starlike pointers flaring from the center of the flower outward to its edge. These characteristic lines of the morning glory are fingered in white.

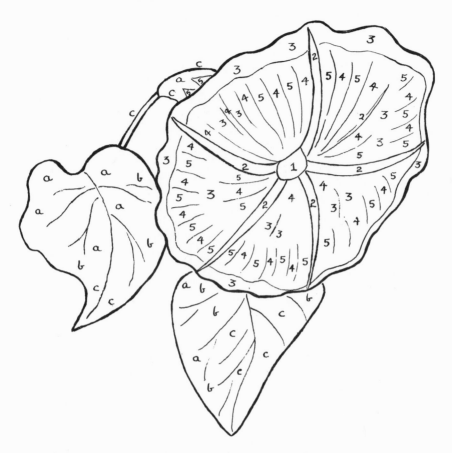

Fig. 46. Blue morning glory pattern. Hook in the following manner: 1, yellow; 2, white; 3, light blue; 4, medium blue; 5, medium dark blue. Leaves are pretty in soft shades from light (a) to dark (c). Veins can be hooked in chartreuse.

Following this step, proceed by adding the remaining shades, 3, 4, and 5, in divisions as illustrated. These lines are hooked in vertical contours, and all point from the center outward to achieve a streaked effect. Always work from the center outward—but as you near the outline, have shade 3 handy to thread among 4 and 5. Short vertical rows of shade 3 intermingled with the darker colorings at the inside edge of the outline will result in better blending.

The upper half of the morning glory varies from the lower part, with longer alternating lines of shades 4 and 5. Thus a darker shadowing on the upper part of the flower is achieved. The lower half features this darker shadowing toward the edge, pointing up shade 3 as a highlight in the center.

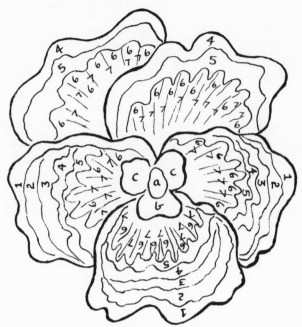

Fig. 47. Yellow and purple pansy pattern. The numbers represent: 1, light yellow; 2, medium yellow; 3, deep yellow; 4, light lavender; 5, medium lavender; 6, purple; 7, deep purple. Centers are hooked as follows: a, light green; b, yellow; c, white.

Although, upon first study, this technique of shading may seem rather tedious, it really is not, and the results are well worth the effort. Once you practice the method of fingering in shades, you are sure to prefer its use for a great number of flowers.

PANSIES

These may be of one coloring, or of two widely contrasting colors. Those with two colors are particular fun to hook. For the example in fig. 47 a yellow and purple flower was chosen.

The center (a, b, c in fig. 47) is always light green, yellow, and white, whatever variation is used for the remaining pansy coloring, and this part of the flower should be hooked first.

The three lower petals are hooked next, since they overlap the two top petals. Each petal is outlined with light yellow, followed by a darker row of yellow within the outline. See 1 and 2 in figs. 47. The next step is to hook a few vertical rows of irregular length, from the center out, using the darkest shade of purple. See 7 in fig. 47. These so-called "whiskers" touch at the pansy center and fan outward into the petal. About six whiskers

Pansy Rug, measuring 52 inches across. The design is by Kathleen Van Wyck, and the rug was hooked by Mrs. D. Vroman. The pansies were "fingered in" (see page 74) with natural colors against a light neutral background of gray-beige. The scroll is in golden yellow shades and the border, dark wine.

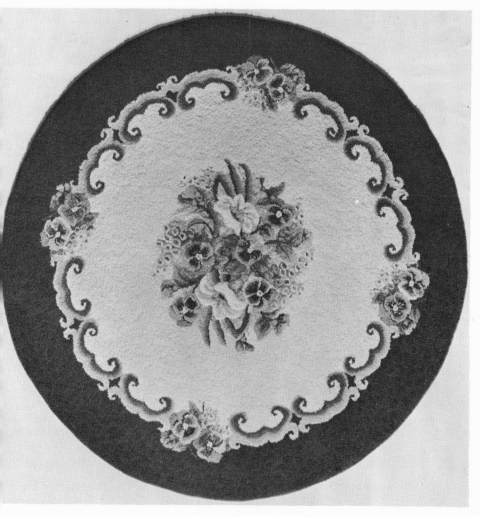

(Photo: Vern Hamilton)

are usually sufficient for medium-sized petals. The next shade lighter purple is used to hook between these whisker lines as shown. The colors to be hooked in wavy horizontal lines across the petals, joining up with the rows of yellow already worked in, are also noted in fig. 47.

The two top petals include the purple and lavender shades only. Each are outlined in the lightest and are completed with the darker shades, as marked in the illustration.

Leaves are worked out in medium- or bronze-green tones. Veins are pretty in light blue-green with stems in a very dark shade.

Other suggested color combinations for the pansy pattern.

Top petals	Bottom petals
Lavender	Blue into lavender
Rusts	Yellow into rust
Rusts	Blue into rust
White into yellows	White into light greens, shading into darker greens

In working out any of these other color combinations, remember that it is always essential to use a very dark shade for whisker lines at the center of the pansy. Unlike most other flowers, lines of vertical shading are imperative.

THE IRIS (fig. 48)

This can be worked out in lavender tones, or it can feature orchid. The latter color may be obtained by adding a small amount of rose or garnet to purple dye.

Yellow or gold irises are also very lovely, especially in a grouping of several blossoms. As in other flowers, the graduated tones of a color series are necessary for an interesting effect.

For added realism, the veining in the lower petals is best hooked in a fuzzy material dyed buttercup yellow. Gray-green leaves should be done from a series of greens in the reseda tones and these need no veining. The stem is hooked in two darker shades of the leaf.

SHADING LEAVES

Leaves are more interesting if their shadings are varied. Some may be made with lighter shades on one side and darker ones on the other; some may be lightest at the tip, shading into dark toward the bottom; others can be dark at the top, shading into light at the base. As in the examples of the flowers, some leaves are more appropriately fingered in for a natural effect. See fig. 49. The first step in following the pattern in the illustration is to establish the veining lines. These should be in a color or shading

78

Fig. 48. Iris pattern. Dye a series in lavender, orchid, or yellow, and hook from lightest shade, 1, to darkest, 6. Hook the center markings on the lower petals in buttercup yellow and the stem in reseda green.

which is of sufficient contrast to the rest of the leaf that they will stand out when the whole leaf has been hooked. Particularly in larger leaves, watch out that the veins are wide enough in the lower part, so that they can taper gracefully toward the tip.

Begin your leaf at the tip with the lightest green—shade 1. First outline the tip, then thread rows of shade 1, running at angles that carry out the same general direction of the veins. Finishing with this shade, start with shade 2, outlining a small part of the outer edge then fingering in rows along the sides of the veining at this section of the leaf. Shade 3 is next carefully fingered in, gradually blending into shade 4, which in turn shades into 5 at the base of the leaf. Alternatively, the leaf could have

Fig. 49. Leaf pattern. Finger in shades of green from lightest, 1, to darkest, 5, as marked.

been begun with dark at the tip, and shaded into the very lightest green at the base, reversing the order of the series. We must remember to vary our leaves slightly as we work, otherwise they may have too hard and uniform a look. The trick here is always to blend or finger in the neighboring shades of green in slightly longer or shorter strips, bringing in a touch of the new shade between two tips of the one you have just finished hooking. In other words, leave tiny pointed spaces where one color leaves off, so that you can thread the next shade into these vacant spaces. With a proper graduated blending of coloring, this manner of shading is extremely pleasing and realistic.

11

THE GROUPING OF FLORAL COLORS

Even though many of today's designs or patterns come with floral colors preplanned, it is frequently advantageous to rearrange them, or perhaps increase or lessen the variation of coloring to suit the room in which the finished rug is to be placed, and also to please the individual hooker's taste. Actually, there are four points to consider when planning floral colors:

1. *Individual taste.* Some people want to work with clear strong colors, and thoroughly enjoy hooking because they feel they can express themselves best with bright shadings. Others find the stronger colors too restless, and prefer soft, subdued colors in their rugs. So the degree and variation of coloring will depend, a great deal, upon the preferences of the individual. It is advisable to consider well the use of rather definite shadings, for time has a way of mellowing all colors. The size of the rug is an important factor, too. If you are hooking a small one, it may be that a bright touch is what is required in the room. On the other hand, if a very large rug is planned, too many bright colors can very well be overpowering. This brings us to the next important point.

2. *The room's colors.* The rug's predominating colors should be chosen to go with the decor of the room for which the rug is planned. This means that the color and type of pattern in the curtains, draperies, upholstery or slipcovers should first be studied. While a rug does not, of course, have to match such decorations exactly, it should at least echo the same colors and introduce new ones only when their effect is generally harmonious. A

major color featured in the room should also figure predominantly in the rug. Thus if the walls are, say, green or white, and the draperies white with a yellow, red, and green pattern, you might choose yellow, red, and green to play a predominant role in the rug, with a gray or beige background, perhaps. You will get many ideas from illustrations of decorator rooms in magazines or books.

3. *Color balance.* To achieve this, you must have more or less equal amounts of coloring in the different parts of your rug. In other words, you would not want to have one half of your rug with blue and lavender flowers, and the other half in red and yellow. Instead, you would alternate warm and cool colors so they were fairly equally distributed all over the pattern. By studying pictures, reproductions, flower arrangements, printed fabrics, needlework, china, and pottery, you will see how designs are balanced for best effects.

4. *Assembly of colors.* For a pleasing collection and arrangement of colors, it is necessary to preplan a floral pattern carefully. Before any hooking is done, consider where to place the colors you want to feature. As the color for each flower is decided upon, mark an X with a corresponding colored crayon directly on the burlap. Needless to say, this will do no harm whatever to the pattern, as the crayon marks will be covered when the rug is hooked. Also, should you change your mind after you have thus identified the colors, you can always alter one or more by crossing off the first X and marking in another color. In this way, you have ample opportunity to study your floral arrangement's coloring thoroughly before any hooking is done. If you are not yet sure enough which colors to mark in, you may find it helpful to cut several small swatches of different colored materials and move these around on the pattern until you arrive at the correct distribution all over the rug. This method also enables you to compare the swatches with the other colors in the room, so the correct shades are arrived at before dyeing a series of strips.

When mapping out your colors in a floral center design, always begin at the center, for this is the main point of interest in your rug. Surrounding floral colors are planned to complement and emphasize the central flower, or grouping, many being worked out in contrasting colors. Although there is no rule about what color the center flower should be, if in doubt as to what to choose, it is usually advisable to select a warm color, such as a red or gold, for one or another shade of either of these will harmonize with just about any color scheme. Among the reds from which to make a selection, there are, of course, the dusty rose tones, the rust tones, or shades of wine. If golds are used, they may vary from a yellowish shade through to mustard gold and the golden browns.

If red is chosen for the center flower, plan a cool color such as blue for the flower nearest to it. The next flower, near the blue, might be hooked in yellow, since a warm color will again be needed. If you chose a shade of gold for the center, you could also have planned blue for the

RED |||||| PINK ||||| YELLOW :::::: YELLOW GREEN ⁒⁒ GREEN ▨ BLUE ☰ MAUVE ⦀

Fig. 50. A good way to plan any color grouping is by marking the flowers and foliage with colored crayons directly on the burlap. The markings at corner of the illustration represent a guide to the different shadings of pink, yellow, green, blue, and mauve chosen for this particular pattern.

second flower, but would now choose one of the red tones (such as pink, shaded with red) for the third blossom.

The fourth flower away from the center might have lavender shading, if it is near a yellow flower, or cream if near a red one. Other smaller surrounding flowers could be in white shading into soft grays, or light greens, with a bright yellow center.

Avoid having flowers of warm colors touching. The same rule applies to the cool shades, such as blue and purple. However, patterns usually come, or are designed, with foliage that separates the flowers, and this often permits harmonious colors in either the cool or warm range to face each other over the green, provided there is a proper overall balance of color. Make sure to repeat the color used in the center flower, even if only in a few smaller flowers around the rug. A good radius would be about the fifth flower from the center, or toward the edge of the grouping.

Generally speaking, floral colors should be stronger toward the center of the rug, and soften toward the outer edge where pink, white, soft blue, yellow, lavender, or other pastel shades are more suitable. When stronger colors are used near the edge to repeat the central color, they should always be in smaller amounts, such as in buds or small flowers. In a multi-floral design containing roses, it is advisable to keep these all in one color, since sufficient contrast is usually afforded by various other flowers in the group. This is a good principle to follow whatever flower is featured in the center of a rug and repeated in smaller versions elsewhere in the pattern.

Leaf colors and shapes are planned according to the flowers accompanying them. However, greens in both cool and warm tones should be repeated in different parts of the rug so that this color, like those in the flowers, is balanced in each part of the design.

While both halves of a rug must be planned with proper respect for color balance, the arrangement should not be identical all the way around, otherwise it will look too set. Next to a red center, for instance, you might plan a lavender flower, and on the opposite side of the center, a blue one. Later on, after placing a similar warm color next to each of them, you might use another lavender flower, this time on the side of the rug where you put the blue one, and put a blue flower in the other half—at a repectful distance from the first lavender one. When you work from the center out in warm and cool colors, your design will have pleasing color harmony and good balance as well. Fig. 50 shows a typical floral center worked out for colors in the method recommended. The different types of marks in the illustration represent different-colored chalks.

If planning colors seems a bit bewildering at first, don't be discouraged, for you will soon see how easy it is in actual practice. Train your eyes to see how color groupings have been arranged in all the woven and painted objects around you, and you'll soon find yourself evolving plenty of ideas of your own.

(Photo: Max Tatch)

Hall runner of pink roses has alternate blocks done in brown tweed mixtures. Hooked by the author.

Hearthrug with broken-wreath motif copied
from a museum pattern about 150 years old.
Note the balance of colors between warm
and cool all over the rug. The patterns for
the roses and grapes are given elsewhere in
this book and can be copied by the reader.
The rug was made by the author for a traditional setting such as shown in the lower
illustration.

Welcome rug for entrance hall or bedroom, hooked by the author. The pattern was taken from an old Dresden plate and the floral colors were matched as closely as possible. Note again the all-over balance of color and the use of a light background. This rug, like the one opposite, was hooked from cut strips of woolen material, some of which were dyed in series as described in chapter 13.

(Photo: Vern Hamilton)

Friendship rug, 19 by 38 inches, made by Opal and Charles Stanick from separate designs sent in by friends.

12

MAKING THE MOST OF WOOLENS ON HAND (BLEACHING, OVERDYEING)

Making the most of your woolens is of primary importance. First, take inventory of what you have on hand by sorting out your colors. Assemble blue woolens in one pile, reds and pinks in another, thus grouping various colors so they may be properly appraised for their color value. The next step is to see if your colors are suitable to complete different color series. To take a popular example—the rose. Suppose six shades were needed for the design, you would classify your red materials as follows:

1. Lightest, a shade of pink, nearly white
2. Next to lightest, shell pink
3. Light rose
4. Dark rose
5. Dark red
6. Wine

While it is most unlikely that all these shadings are on hand, it is surprising how easily they can be assembled. If you have rose- and wine-colored material, it is entirely possible to complete the above color series by a gentle bleaching in soap suds, followed by a thorough rinsing. This can result in your six shades of red.

BLEACHING BY SIMMERING

Let's start with some of the rose material in our example. You will find that the time required for simmering depends upon the shade desired, the lighter shades requiring the longest treatment.

Take one strip of rose material, place in a pan of boiling soapy water and stir until it reaches the lightest shade required by the series. When that one is finished, simmer another strip for a shorter time, so that it will make the second, slightly darker, shade you need. The third shade may take very little bleaching. The fourth shade is the natural rose color of the material. For the fifth shade, bleach out a strip from the wine-colored material in the same manner as you did for the lighter rose shades. If there seems too much variation between the bleached wine shade and the original (darkest) rose shade, the latter material may be simmered along with a wine strip, thus making the two materials closer in coloring. Finally, the wine material in its natural coloring is used for the darkest shade. In this way, strips for six shades, making up a color series, are gained from only two colors of material.

You will now see how simple it is to take but a few colored materials that are on hand, and without dyeing, accumulate a good collection of color series. One word of advice, however, is in order. Be sure to stir materials continuously while simmering, otherwise you will end up with streaked colors. These are not good in a color series, for our effect is planned with separate strips of different shades rather than with variations in any one strip. Slightly streaked strips can be used once in a while, if a mistake has been made, but too many will tend to take away from the desired effect.

COMMERCIAL BLEACHES FOR BLEACHING WHITE

There are very good bleaches on the market that do a fine job of changing colors into white or neutral shades. When using established brands, no boiling is necessary. A package of bleach will do one pound or one yard of most woolens. Occasionally some dark colors won't bleach properly, so when white is desired it is usually best to concentrate on the lighter shades of materials you have on hand.

HOW TO USE COMMERCIAL BLEACHES

The first step in bleaching is to dissolve bleach powder in cool water. Place enough water in the pan so that the strips of material, when inserted, will be completely covered and so that they can be stirred around easily.

Before placing the material in the bleaching pan, wash and rinse it thoroughly. Next, add the strips to the bleach solution, lifting and stirring constantly. Gradually heat to just under boiling point, continuing to lift and stir until the color has been removed. This may take 5 minutes. Be sure not to let the solution boil. After bleaching, wash and rinse the material thoroughly. If the color is not sufficiently removed on all the strips, repeat the bleaching procedure once more.

BLEACHING WITH AMMONIA

Good results are often achieved with ammonia added to water. Even though the colored strips may not bleach out quite white, they can be lightened and softened when placed in this solution and simmered. Use 1 teaspoon of ammonia to 1 quart of water, and simmer material from 15 to 30 minutes on a burner, stirring all the while. Use sufficient water to cover material, and a large enough vessel so that the material won't be crowded while stirred. After bleaching, rinse material thoroughly and allow to dry.

BEIGES, TANS, GRAYS, AND DARK COLORS

Light-colored materials such as beiges, tans, soft grays are usually most suited for background use, since they blend with all colors, and allow floral arrangements to show up against them to the best advantage. It is usually wise, therefore, to preserve the neutral colors for just this purpose. Very dark shades of green, brown, wine, as well as black, are often just right for borders, so it's a good idea to check all the colors you are going to need before starting in bleaching or dyeing any material into other shades.

OVERDYEING

Often you can overdye colored woolens you have on hand to make suitable shades in a color series. This is a practical and economical process, since overdyed colors offer many shading possibilities. A chart follows showing what color variations overdyeing produces.

COLOR CHART FOR OVERDYEING

	Over Red Produces	Over Blue Produces	Over Yellow Produces	Over Brown Produces	Over Orange Produces	Over Green Produces	Over Purple Produces
RED	darker red	purple	scarlet	red-brown	light red	soft brown	reddish purple
BLUE	purple	dark blue	green	dark brown	dull dark gray	bottle green	bluish purple
YELLOW	scarlet	green	dark yellow	golden brown	yellow-orange	light green	greenish brown
BROWN	brownish red	nearly black	yellow-brown	darker brown	warm dark brown	dull greenish brown	chocolate
GREEN	nearly black	greenish blue	yellow-green	olive green	myrtle green	dark green	dull dark green
ORANGE	light red	dull dark gray	lighter orange	tobacco brown	dark orange	yellow green	reddish brown
PURPLE	reddish purple	plum	nearly black	dark reddish brown	dull purple	dull dark purple	dark purple

ADDITIONAL NOTES ON OVERDYEING LIGHT SHADES

Yellow over pink produces—apricot.
Yellow over light blue produces—light green.
Yellow over light green produces—chartreuse.
Pink over blue produces—lavender.
Pink over beige produces—rose beige.
Lavender over light gray produces—dull lavender.
Small amount of golden brown over white produces—antique white.
Small amount of golden brown over beige produces—tan.
Green over gray produces—gray green.
Green over tan produces—bronze-green.
Green over gold produces—bright moss green.
Gray plus green over black produces—antique black.

13

DYEING A COLOR SERIES—FOR
FLOWERS AND LEAVES

Only at first will the beginner be satisfied to use
materials that are handy in ready-made colors, for in making a really beautiful floral rug, sooner or later it becomes necessary to dye one or more
color series. By employing a system for dyeing, you will find it a simple
procedure and almost as much fun as hooking.

NECESSARY EQUIPMENT FOR DYEING

1. *Enamel or aluminum pan* (wash basin for small amount of woolens,
or a larger vessel for dyeing larger quantities).
2. *Dyes in required colors.*
3. *Salt to set the dye solution.* (Noniodized ice cream salt is good.)
4. *Measuring spoons.*
5. *Long-handle fork, spoon, or stick*—to stir and turn woolens.
In addition, you will need hot water for simmering and cool water for
rinsing.

SELECTING MATERIALS TO DYE FOR FLOWERS

Save your choice flannel scraps of white or cream to dye for flowers
and leaves—or procure such material from a rummage sale or mill-end
shop. Most hookers use their best flannel strips for roses, as these flowers
so often predominate in the floral grouping. If short on white, use light
pink for pink or red roses. A yellow or gold series may be dyed over faded
yellow material, with the exception of the two lighter shades which must
be dyed over white. Blue flower series can be dyed over faded blues, while

lavenders can be obtained by dyeing over light grays, as well as over faded materials of the same color. Greens for leaves may be dyed over lighter greens, beiges, grays, tans, as well as white or creams. Naturally the color over which you dye will influence the final shade of your strips.

GETTING EVERYTHING READY

1. Woolens to be dyed must be *clean*, and should have all seams ripped apart. Material is torn into strips around 4 inches wide and 18 to 24 inches long. Whether one or more strips is needed will depend upon the size of the detail to be hooked in that particular color. Supplementary flowers and leaves may take rather less, per unit.

2. Assemble all the colored dyes you need for your series.

3. Rubber gloves. These are not essential, but will prevent staining hands while dyeing.

4. Though many craftsmen use vinegar for setting colors, the writer prefers salt, since the chemical reaction of vinegar sometimes changes colors to queer off-tones. Noniodized salt never changes the color tone, yet does an equally good job of making the colors permanent.

5. *Before starting to dye, strips must be thoroughly soaked and wrung out.*

6. The average color series for five or six medium-sized flowers uses a half package of dye, dissolved in a small casserole dish. Pour half a cup of boiling water over the dye and stir thoroughly.

DYEING THE SERIES (figs. 51 and 52)

First strip. Dye your lightest shade first. Take ½ teaspoon of the dissolved liquid dye and add to 1 quart of warm or hot water in a pan. Place over a low flame or burner. (Do not use a galvanized pan, for its chemical reaction prevents dyeing.) After adding the dye, stir water before putting in your strip of woolen. When it is hot and before it starts to simmer, add damp strip, stir again, sprinkling salt generously in the dye bath. Continue simmering and stirring strip until it has absorbed dye and water is almost clear. This shade will be very light. Rinse strip until water runs clear. Squeeze out excess water, fold strip and lay nearby for convenient comparison when the next strip is dyed.

Second strip. For the second shade, double the amount of liquid dye used for the first strip—in other words, add 1 teaspoon liquid dye to the same amount of water. Follow procedure as for the first shade, simmering with additional salt until the color is absorbed. Rinse, and lay folded strip next to the first, where the colors can be compared.

Remaining strips. Each of the succeeding shades are made in a similar way, by doubling the amount of dye used on the previous one, and adding more salt each time. Thus by using ½ teaspoon of dye for the first shade,

94

Fig. 51. Equipment needed for dyeing a color series. Always dye the lightest tint first, adding more dye for each deeper shade required. Note the handy container for salt.

1 teaspoon for the second, 2 teaspoons for the third, 4 teaspoons for the fourth, 8 teaspoons for the fifth, and 16 teaspoons for the sixth, a series of six shades is accumulated.

You will find the materials take the dye differently, so it is advisable to keep close watch, the idea being to let the strips simmer long enough only to arrive at an equal color variation. It may sometimes be necessary, therefore, to remove certain of the strips from the pan before they absorb all the dye. Keep comparing new strips with those already done, so that you arrive at a good even series. Remember that colors will appear darker when wet. When strips are taken out before all the dye is absorbed, allowances must be made before additional dye is added.

Very dark shades, such as those needed for the two darkest tones of a deep red rose, can be achieved by the addition of a little black dye. For the next to last shade, use $\frac{1}{16}$ teaspoon of black, and for the darkest shade, $\frac{1}{8}$ teaspoon. The black is in addition to the usual formula of red in both cases. Although the black dye need not be dissolved before adding to the

95

Fig. 52. As right tints or shades are obtained, remove strips from basin with fork, rinse thoroughly in cold water, fold and place nearby so colors may be compared.

hot water already in the dye bath, it must be thoroughly dissolved along with the other dye before any material is immersed. The addition of black dye is recommended not only for the example given, but for any coloring where a very dark shade is required. Very large leaves, for instance, designed in numerous shades, may call for black in the darkest shades—and you will undoubtedly find other occasions for its use. Naturally, the darker the coloring the longer the simmering period required.

NATURAL COLORS FOR THE DARKEST SHADES

Many times it is unnecessary to dye dark shades in leaves and flowers, since the hooker will often have dark greens, wines, and other strong-colored materials on hand. These shades are often richer and lovelier in tone than any you can dye, even with much effort. It also saves in time and the cost of dye to keep, or secure, any dark natural colors such as old wine-color bath robes, dark green flannel skirts, or dark brown slacks.

LEFTOVER DYE

If you end up with perfectly good dissolved dye in the pan, don't throw it away. Placed in small mayonnaise jars, it can be properly labeled for future use and will keep indefinitely.

MAKING NOTES

Whenever your dyeing is turning out unusually well, it's worth while to make notes on exact procedures, how much dye was used, what color it was dyed over, etc., for memories have a way of tricking us all. Such notes come in handy over and over again.

SUGGESTED DYES FOR FLOWERS AND LEAVES

Pink into red roses:	Garnet or old rose dye
Deep red roses:	2 parts garnet, 1 part cardinal, ⅛ teaspoon turkey red
Yellow roses:	Gold dye for first 3 shades, followed by shades dyed from 3 parts gold to 1 part golden brown, using brown for darkest
Bluebells:	Sky blue dye
Pansies:	Any color dye desired, particularly in shades of yellow, lavender, purple
Iris:	Purple, or 2 parts purple to 1 part blue
Daisies:	Same as yellow roses, or purple dye
Regal lilies:	Pink, apricot, or light green dye
Poppies:	Scarlet, rust, or gold dye
Morning glories:	Blue dye, or 2 parts blue, 1 part purple
Jonquils:	Same as yellow roses
Tulips:	Same as yellow or red roses, or purple
Leaves for lavender flowers:	Chartreuse or silver-green dye
Leaves for tulips, irises, or poppies:	Equal parts of jade green and gray dye
Rose leaves:	Bronze-green, or 3 parts medium green to 1 part gold dye
Leaves for yellow flowers:	Bright green dye, or bronze-green
Leaves for blue flowers:	Jade, or bright green

In addition to these dye colors, remember that many flowers can be hooked in neutral-colored white, cream, beige material, etc., instead of in their natural colors.

14

DYEING FOR GRAPES, SCROLLS, BACKGROUNDS, BORDERS

GRAPES

Series of colors for grapes are dyed in similar manner to those for flowers and leaves. The following shadings are popular:

1. *Purple.* This color series may be dyed over white, light gray, or beige material—fine smooth flannel being the best for the purpose, if you can get it. Using purple dye, you can make anywhere from 5 to 8 shades, from almost white to a very deep shade.

2. *Green.* Your series in this color can be dyed over very light yellow or green, beige or white flannel. For the lighter shades, use equal parts of green and yellow dye. For the remaining shades add slightly more green to the dye left over, continuing the series into a very dark green.

3. *Blue* grapes are pretty when made from 3 parts blue to 1 part purple dye, in a color series from very light to dark. This color dyes well over light gray or beige as well as white, the latter being necessary for the lightest shade.

4. *Pink* grapes are shaded in the lavender rose tones, to resemble Tokay grapes. Mix equal parts of purple and rose dye for coloring light beige, gray, pink, or white flannel.

Spirals near grape clusters. Make these curved lines from the light tones used in the green grape series. Some may be darker than others.

Grape stems. Dye 2 shades of golden brown for the stems of any colored grapes, so the natural color in the vine is approximately matched.

SCROLLS

Color series for scrolls in a rug design are dyed in very much the same manner as flower or leaf series. A typical three-color series would need a light, medium, and a dark shade. The usual rule of thumb is to double the quantity of dye for each shade, though much will depend on the type and color of the materials used—a very wide choice of woolens being possible for this part of the rug.

Be sure, as always, to check through all the material you have on hand before planning to dye a scroll series. Remember, too, that light material can be dyed to darker shades and dark materials can be boiled out to lighter colors. Be sure you have enough material on hand for all the scrolls before you start dyeing. Consider checks and plaids for veinings as well as plain-colored materials.

BACKGROUNDS

Tinting light materials. A great number of rugs call for a medium- to light-toned background. Very often the hooker will have enough material on hand, or will buy mill ends in an appropriate color so that dyeing is not necessary for large expanses of hooking. However, sometimes it is not possible to come by just the right shade, or it is necessary to use up material on hand.

Taking the lightest background into consideration first, you may want a soft *antique white.* This is best obtained from tinting pure-white material with a weak solution of golden-brown dye, following the soaking method of dyeing described shortly. With different dyes, any *pastel shade* can be produced for a background such as soft greens, blues, and pinks.

Beige is a popular color both in clothing and in rug backgrounds. This can sometimes be hooked as is, or if too light, a darker tint may easily be obtained. Using this as a typical example, an average-sized full-length coat might require no more than a ¼ teaspoonful of dark brown dye added to sufficient water to tint the entire coat, before cutting it into strips.

Material to be tinted may be simmered with salt, as described in chapter 13, or it can be soaked in the following way without simmering: First, dissolve dye in a small amount of boiling water, then add dissolved mixture to very hot water, enough to cover the material in the pan. Be sure to stir the hot dye water thoroughly before adding the material (well soaked and wrung out) to be dyed. Add plenty of salt to the solution and keep the material in the pan for about 5 minutes, or until the water cools, stirring all the while with a long-handled fork or stick.

After soaking in dye water, material must be thoroughly rinsed in cold water. This aids in setting the color. If you find the color is not as strong as desired, repeat the operation, adding slightly more dye to the hot water. Always bear in mind that the color will appear about three shades darker when wet than it will when dry. It is therefore wise for the beginner to let the material dry before judging its shading.

The soaking method of tinting is recommended for dyeing light shades, and is particularly convenient for large quantities of material, sizable amounts being awkward to handle. A shorter or longer time may be required for the material in the dye bath, according to the strength of the mixture and the shade desired. If in doubt, it is wise to use rather less dye for your solution, so the material can first be tested, and more dye added later if needed.

Dark colors for backgrounds or borders definitely require the other method of dyeing. Use a handful of salt with a large amount of material in a strong dye solution. Simmer or boil until the desired shade is reached, as described in chapter 13, stirring all the while, and follow by rinsing several times in fresh water—until no color comes out of the material. For a very dark color, add a little black to the other dye.

15

SPOT DYEING FOR AUTUMN LEAVES, FLOWERS, FRUITS

It is really fun to dye material in different shades by the easy method of spot dyeing. No separate color series are needed here, as different colors are dyed on the same strip. When hooked into a pattern the multicolored leaves (or flowers and fruits) can look most effective and realistic.

MATERIALS TO USE

Any *light* shade of woolen material such as beige, yellow, gold, white, cream, pink, light green, or blue is fine for spot dyeing. Old faded materials are just as good as even-toned ones, and either thin or thick woolens can be used, whichever is handiest.

THE SIZE OF THE STRIPS

It is best to use long strips for spot dyeing, such as the length of a pair of white flannel trousers, so that three or four colors may be spot dyed on the single length. This is about equal to a 36-inch strip. The width of the strip may vary, but 4 to 8 inches is convenient to handle and affords a generous strip of spot-dyed material. This can be cut into narrower strips later on for hooking.

DYES FOR AUTUMN LEAVES

You can use almost any color dye in the brighter shades, particularly the reds, greens, golds, golden browns, yellows. In the reds, the rust tones, cardinal and turkey reds, or the rose or garnet shades work out excellently. Among the greens, Nile, jade, olive, or bronze tones are all good. Add to this the wide range of yellows from light through dark mustard and the browns. Blue and purple are not used much, except for some of the shadings in grape leaves.

HOW TO START (figs. 53 and 54)

Wet material thoroughly and squeeze out excess water. Put from ½ to 1 cup of water (depending on width of strip to be dyed) in an enamel or aluminum wash basin. Place over slow heat and put about 8 or 10 inches of the long strip in the warm water, crushing the immersed part and leaving it wrinkled in a pile in the basin. The water should never cover the material, but instead, come up part way over woolen. The remaining part of the strip lies outside the pan during the first operation.

Having chosen your color dye for the end of the strip, sprinkle the dry dye *sparingly* on the material without stirring. Follow this immediately by sprinkling *generously* with salt. Allow to simmer without stirring until water has all but boiled dry. About 3 or 4 minutes is usually sufficient unless material is extra heavy, in which case simmer slightly longer. Take off heat and thoroughly rinse dyed part of strip with cold water.

The second color. Choose another color dye, and repeat the above operation, starting with the part of the strip adjoining the section just dyed. Leave the ends hanging over the pan. Fresh warm or hot water is used for each color. Be sure to use contrasting colors as you proceed along the strip with different dyes. Thus you may have green, brown, yellow, and red equally proportioned on the same strip. With each new color, it is prettier if you overlap the previous shading slightly at the edge. This will effect a better blending.

DON'TS IN SPOT DYEING

Don't use too much water. Don't use too much dye, or dump a big batch in one spot. Spread or scatter more or less evenly. Don't try spot dyeing dark materials as it won't turn out satisfactorily. Don't be afraid of bright colors. Don't try to get too many colors on one strip, or shadings will be overcrowded when worked up. Not more than eight inches of each color is recommended for large leaves, and rather less for smaller leaves.

Fig. 53. Method of spot dyeing. One end of strip (first soaked in water) is crushed into wrinkles and placed in shallow water. Dye is then sprinkled in powder form from a spoon so color is variegated on each strip. Left illustration shows the sprinkling of a second color, the end at right having already been treated.

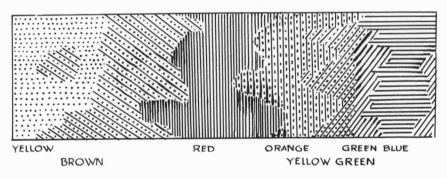

YELLOW   RED   ORANGE   GREEN BLUE
    BROWN   YELLOW GREEN

Fig. 54. A spot-dyed strip in variegated colors from green through rust, red, brown, and gold. The different shadings in the illustration represent different colors.

SPOT DYEING OVER COLORED MATERIALS FOR AUTUMN LEAVES

Over yellow or gold: Spot dye with Nile green, cardinal, golden brown, and brown.

Over light blue: Spot dye with gold, green, turkey red, and yellow.

Over white or gray: Spot dye with rose, jade green, gold, and olive green.

Over pink: Spot dye with bright green, garnet, gold, and brown.

Over light green: Spot dye with gold, olive green, apricot, and yellow.

Always spot dye material so that some of the original colors show through in places.

SPOT DYEING ROSE LEAVES

Beautiful rose leaves may be spot dyed over coral or a terra cotta colored material. Unlike autumn leaves, a shorter strip is crushed down into shallow water, and just one shade of dye in a bright green is sprinkled carefully over the entire strip. Sprinkle salt generously over material while simmering. Coral or terra cotta highlights will shine through the green spot dyeing in a most attractive manner.

SPOT DYEING FOR FORGET-ME-NOTS

Groupings of tiny forget-me-nots look enchanting when hooked with light blue material spot-dyed with garnet or American beauty dye. Follow same procedure as for the rose leaves, but with the different dye.

SPOT DYEING FOR PEACH, PEAR, AND PLUM

When a pattern calls for yellow-toned pears or peaches, spot dye yellow material with a little scarlet dry dye. This will achieve a pinky tone to highlight the cheeks of the fruit. For the plum (purple) dye material light blue for lightest highlight, then spot dye darker shades, using lavender dye with a bit of red added.

Modern Rose, 38 by 62 inches, designed by Willa Gaskill and hooked by Gertrude Manuel.

(Photo: Vern Hamilton)

Autumn Leaves. Hooked by Anna Grisham, this rug is done in the true autumn colors of gold, rust, green, brown, and yellow.

16

HOW TO HOOK WITH SPOT-DYED MATERIALS

HOOKING AUTUMN LEAVES

Hooking autumn leaves is so fascinating that every hooker should include at least one such rug in her collection. There are practically no shading problems when the strips are spot dyed in fall colors as described in the previous chapter.

Veins should be hooked first, and in a strong color such as brown, dark green, or purple. They may vary for different autumn leaves in the same rug—in which case choose a vein color that offers the greatest contrast. In large leaves, veins should be hooked in a fine double row, tapering into a single row toward each end. See fig. 55.

The autumn leaf itself is started by hooking the outline with a long spot-dyed strip. If your strip runs out before you finish the outline, cut another one and continue with the same rotation of color, but in reverse. In other words, suppose your strip begins with gold at the base of the leaf (next to stem), changing to green, red, and then brown, your second strip would continue the outline with brown, changing to red, green, and then gold. If additional strips are still needed, continue the outline in the same manner, starting with the same color with which you ended the previous strip. Your coloring will now be mapped out for the completion of the leaf. (N.B. Small leaves may take only 2 or 3 colors on a strip to complete the outline, but the same principle is followed.)

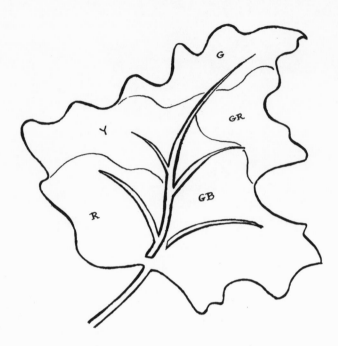

Fig. 55. Autumn leaf pattern. Y represents yellow; G, gold; GR, green; GB, golden brown; R, red. Veins can be hooked in either dark brown, dark green, or purple; with stem in golden brown.

Additional rows are now hooked inside the leaf pattern, using the same colored strips and method as for the outline. There may be room for three or four contour rows between the outline and the ends of the veining. When you come to the veined section, it will be necessary to hook between the veins, following their direction rather than the outer contour of the leaf. Each section between the veins should match the color of the outer part of the leaf at the point where the rows meet. This means that in each case you will use only the part of the spot-dyed strip that matches the outer edge. Here you will need to cut your strips apart and hook correspondingly shorter rows in the same color. As you move around between the veining, you will of course be using all the different colors you have cut apart and segregated. By keeping the colors consistent from the edge to the center, your leaf will have smoother and more attractive shading. Sometimes just a little color from the adjoining part of the leaf is carried over to the next veined area for a more blended effect. This touch of coloring is hooked quite near the base of the vein and usually some half-dozen loops are sufficient. The latter shading is entirely optional, but it does break up a solid color in an attractive and natural-looking way.

BALANCING AUTUMN LEAVES IN A BORDER

In a rug with an autumn-leaf border, keep your leaves balanced by matching the colors in opposite positions as much as possible. The leaves may never, of course, turn out to be exact duplicates, nor should you strive for this, but they should be made from the same dyed strip—or another one dyed in the same tones. Also, it is best to alternate colors in neighboring leaves around the border. For instance, if you have a leaf with rust tones predominating on one side, the adjoining leaf should feature contrasting colors, such as green or gold, nearest to the rust of the adjoining leaf. If one leaf seems bold in coloring, complement it with one less colorful nearby.

HOOKING ROSE LEAVES FROM SPOT-DYED STRIP

First of all, vein the leaf with dark rust or brown. Cut through the length of apricot material spot dyed with green, as described in the previous chapter, and hook the outline of the entire leaf. Repeat the outline with a contour line within the first row, and continue in this manner, filling in around the leaf until reaching tips of veins. The inner parts of the leaf are filled in with rows slanting the same way as the veins. If the material was evenly mottled by the dyeing procedure, your leaf will have attractive, well-balanced flecks of green and coral—very different in effect from leaves made with a color series. In any individual grouping, keep to one or the other method, using either spot-dyed material or a color series, but not both.

HOOKING FORGET-ME-NOTS FROM SPOT-DYED STRIP

Make tiny center for each flower with a couple of bright yellow loops. Cut your spot-dyed strip into the usual widths for hooking and start with the small petals, some of which will come blue, some garnet, and yet others a blending of the two tones as one, if the strip was dyed as suggested in chapter 15. Try to make the petals of the different flowers contrast where they touch, so as to make each flower stand out individually. A shadowing of a dull dark green or purple may be used to fill in remaining spaces between flowers.

17

HOW TO SHADE VARIOUS FRUITS

While fruit may be a new idea to many hookers, it was very popular in the rugs of long ago. One of the most charming traditional designs is the grape and autumn-leaf motif. The writer had so much fun making her first rug with this design that it wasn't long before three had been worked out in different variations, one of them being chosen for a color illustration in a leading home magazine. The number of enthusiastic letters received as a result proved that there is still more than a local interest in this type of pattern.

GRAPES (fig. 56)

Whether you are hooking grapes in green, purple, blue, or in pink and lavender, the shading technique is the same. One of the most important points to remember is to be consistent with highlights and shadows. Any good picture of the subject will illustrate this consistency. It is advisable to cut materials very fine, so that more shades may be included. This will result in better contours—or a natural roundness to each fruit. If your lightest shade isn't almost white, better use white for the highlight.

First outline the lower part of the grape in the darkest grape shade of your color series. This line, representing the deepest shadow, should encircle about half of the grape, perhaps a little less. Next use the third from lightest shade to complete the outline. Follow the third shade by hooking the second lightest shade directly underneath. Now you are ready

Autumn Glory features fruits and sweet corn in a cornucopia. The rug, in natural colors and dark border, measures 52 inches in diameter and was designed and hooked by Nova Lee, a former pupil of the author.

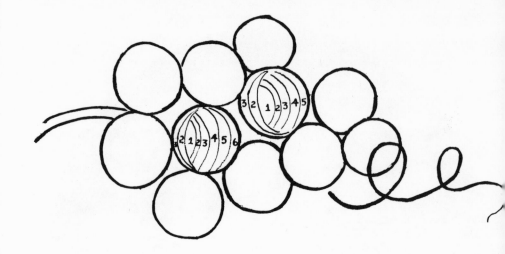

Fig. 56. Grape pattern. Use a color series in any one of the following: green, purple, violet, or pink-lavender. Hook graduated shades from light, 1, to darkest shade, 6, as indicated. Stem is hooked in golden brown, spirals at right in yellow-green.

to put in a spot of the lightest shade (or white) for the highlight. This will take 3 or 4 loops in a close round grouping. After the highlight, it is just a matter of shading the rest of the grape from light to dark, using about four more shades, including the darkest which you first hooked around the lower contour of the grape. All the rows below the highlight should be done in circular lines. Work out your rows to accommodate each shade, as you work down toward the dark outline. There may not be room for more than one row of each color, getting progressively darker as you work down. Make each grape the same way, realizing that the larger ones may include more shades (or more rows of one color) than the smaller ones. There will be small spaces left in the center of the pattern between the individual grapes. These can be filled in with a very dark color to represent a shadowed background. The coloring used for these background areas will depend on the color of the grapes. For purple grapes a dark violet-blue looks well. For blue grapes, use navy blue; for green grapes, a dark forest green is usually best, while pink and lavender grapes are nicely offset by a wine-colored background. All these colors are planned so that the grapes will stand out in the pattern. In principle, however, use such background sparingly, for too much shadowing detracts from the alive beauty of the fruit. In other words, make sure that the grapes touch each other in many places, as shown in fig. 56, so that the background has only to be hooked in small areas. Grape stems are best hooked in golden brown, and spiraling tendrils in light yellow-green.

RED APPLES (fig. 57)

To make an apple, do the stem first, using dark brown or black. Next hook the highlights and shadows before attempting to fill in. Make your shadow lines by hooking a circular row of the wine color near the stem as shown in fig. 57, and another row of the same color curving from the lower part of the apple near the edge, going about halfway up. Make another wine row on the opposite side near the edge of the top curve of the apple, and a fourth shadow line, curving near the center of the cheek. All these shadow lines follow the contour line of the apple as shown in the illustration.

For the highlights, use light yellow or white. Make a short light line on each side of the stem where it goes into the apple, extending about ½ inch on one side, and slightly less on the other. Then add 2 or 3 more loops to complete this highlight area indicated in fig. 57. Other highlights are a curved line at the upper-right side of the apple, spaced about the fourth line in from the edge; a curving line below the stem at center; and a couple of short highlights of 2 or 3 loops each just to the left of the center. This will be about sufficient highlighting and the apple can then be completed by outlining and filling in with red.

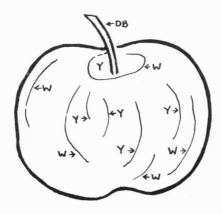

Fig. 57. Apple pattern. Hook highlights and shadows marked as follows: DB, dark brown; Y, light yellow; W, wine. The oval at base of stem should be very light yellow or cream. Then fill in rest of apple with red.

Fig. 58. Strawberry pattern. Hook stems in brown. Leaflets on stems are outlined with medium green and filled in with light green. The freckles should be in antique white or yellow-white, the rest of the berry in scarlet. For a partly ripe berry fill in the right area marked in the lower illustration with light greenish cream, the center area with pinkish orange, and the left area in scarlet.

STRAWBERRIES (fig. 58)

Small, light dots, or freckles, are the characteristic markings of a straw-berry, and these should be hooked in first. Use light yellow or white ma-terial, and hook 1 loop for each spot, cutting the thread each time. Hook the stem next in dark green or brown, then do the small stem leaves over-lapping the berry. Outline these first in darkish green, then fill in with lighter green. Follow this step by outlining the entire strawberry in scarlet red, filling in half of the area around the freckles from edge to center with a light pinkish red. Next hook a couple of rows of darker pink and finish filling in the berry with the scarlet used for the outline. Other berries may vary in shading by having less of the pinkish red shading and more of the scarlet to fill in. On some, the pinkish red could be in the center part, with darker scarlet shades on each side. Still other strawberries could be filled in entirely with scarlet.

CHERRIES (fig. 59)

Hook the stems first in light brown, then add 2 or 3 loops of wine color where the stem joins the fruit. Underline the wine color with a very light pink or white ring as indicated in fig. 59. Emphasize the highlight with 3 or 4 additional loops in a short row underneath the ring.

Next outline the entire cherry in wine color. Then from the highlight down, with rows following the contour of the cherry, shade from light in graduating shades to dark at the base.

Vary a cluster of cherries by outlining others in an intermediate shade —about two shades lighter than wine. In the latter case, the darkest line of wine falls across the center of the cherry. Highlights are hooked at the base of the stem as before, but the part directly underneath the highlight shades quickly into dark, with one intermediary shade between it and the wine across the center. Use a shade lighter than wine underneath this dark center row, finishing with the same shade as used for the outline of this variation.

Fig. 59. Cherry pattern. Hook circle around stem of cherry in dark wine, 4, with a half circle of light pink for highlight directly below this shading, then hook remaining areas as follows: 2, next to lightest shade of wine; 3, medium wine; 4, dark wine. Outline cherry in dark wine. The illustration at right shows a variation when clusters are used. Use the following colors: 1, lightest pink; 3, lighter wine; 4, dark wine. Stems are hooked in brown.

BANANAS (fig. 60)

The stem of the banana consists of a nub of black, made by hooking about 4 loops. The end is also a spot of black, made with 3 loops. Circle the end with light green as indicated in fig. 60. To shade a banana realistically you will need two rows to represent ridges. These rows, hooked in brown and tan, run lengthwise, dividing the banana into three equal parts as shown in the illustration. Outline banana in yellow, and complete it by filling in with the same color.

Fig. 60. Banana pattern. Hook oval at top end of banana in black, also circle at other end, with rings of light green. Center ridges down length of banana (outlined) can be hooked in brown. The upper of these two ridges can be broken with tan for about a third of the length as indicated by dotted lines. Fill areas between outlines with yellows.

When using several bananas in a pattern, vary some of them by filling in with two or three shades of yellow. One part may thus be lighter than the part between the adjoining ridges.

PLUMS (fig. 61)

First plan your highlights of white and light lavender-pink on either side of the dark lavender center. The lower part of the plum is finished off in medium and dark shades of reddish purple. The upper parts of the plum at and near the contour lines are of darker lavender-pink, completing the contour of the plum. Stems are hooked in fine lines of brown and green.

PEARS (fig. 62)

The stem is hooked in a light and dark shade of golden brown. The blossom part of the pear at the opposite end is made with a small spot of loops in black, outlines with rust and finally with a circle of white as indicated in fig. 62. Next work the highlight on the wide center of the pear, making a round spot in a light pink to apricot shade. This highlight con-

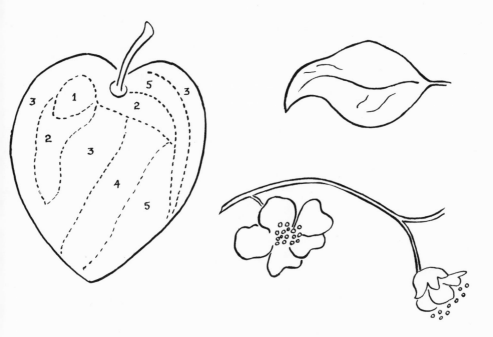

Fig. 61. Plum pattern. Fruit colors are: 1, white; 2, light lavender-pink; 3, darker lavender-pink; 4, medium red-purple; 5, dark red-purple. The blossom is shaded white with gray edges. Dots of orange, yellow, and a little green are hooked at the center. Stem consists of a line of green and one of brown. Leaves are light and medium green with an occasional streak of brown. Veins are dark green.

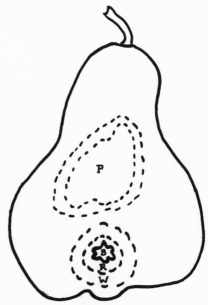

Fig. 62. Pear pattern. Hook center highlight, P, in light pink-apricot, and surround with antique white or very light pink within dotted area. The lower marking is worked in black, B, rust, R, and Antique white, W. Hook stem in a row each of light and dark golden brown. Fill in rest of pear in yellows from a medium at edges to lighter yellow near center.

117

sists of several loops, the number depending upon the size of the pear. Increase the size of the highlight on both sides by adding two additional rows of lightest pink or white. Outline·the pear with light golden brown and fill in the remaining space with yellows, shading from darker hues at the outline to lighter shades on each side of the highlight.

For variation, other pears may shade from light at the outline into darkest yellows surrounding the highlight. The highlights may be the same, or else use a light pink-apricot for this central area, omitting the lightest pink or white used in the first example.

OTHER FRUITS

Shadings of other fruits can be done in a similar manner to the examples given here. Always remember that *highlights* and *shadows* are the making of realistic fruit. With just a few such touches in the right places, your fruit will come alive. Study actual fruit, also paintings and illustrations which can be an endless source of inspiration. The introduction of white into a highlight is always a good procedure if in doubt as to whether any other shade will show up sufficiently well.

18

SCROLLS CAN MAKE OR BREAK

Scrolls play a major role in traditional rug styles. And they may be simple or elaborate, depending on the type and size of rug. Small rugs usually look better with simple scrolls, whereas larger rugs with wider borders can have as fanciful a scroll motif as you like. The most popular scrolls come under one of the following classifications:

1. *Scrolls forming a modest, unobtrusive frame* for a center floral grouping.
2. *Scrolls sharing the importance of the pattern in the center.*
3. *Scrolls dominating the pattern*—either accompanying a few flowers or comprising the sole decoration of the rug.

Apart from the size and style of a scroll, there must be a relationship in color between this frame and the central design. In the first classification, for instance, the color used in some of the leaves of a center pattern may suggest an appropriate green to repeat in the scroll design. Or yellow and gold daisies used in the center might indicate a soft gold scroll—one of the most popular of all colors. Again, red roses might call for a muted rose scroll shading from pale pink into dark wine. The modest scroll would be of muted colorings, allowing the center arrangement to be the predominant attraction of the rug. In other words, the scroll purposely takes second place.

The scroll in the second classification may include more or stronger color, since it shares the importance of the central pattern. While its colors

Fig. 63. A simple scroll design.

should not be garish or harsh, they need not be as muted or grayed in tone as the scrolls in the first classification. Again scroll colors are best if chosen from the center grouping, so both are properly related.

In the third classification, the scroll is planned first, as the main design feature of the rug. Any flowers or other accompanying details are planned as secondary elements, to play up the scroll's importance. Many a handsome rug has been hooked with a decorative scroll on a plain-colored contrasting background.

NARROW SCROLLS

The narrow scroll at most needs only three shades of a single color— light, medium, and dark. The light shade should be used on the outer edge, the dark on the inside edge, while the medium shade acts as a blender between the two. There should be about the same variation of tone among the three shades. By hooking the lightest color first, then the darkest, it is easier to space the in-between shade properly.

WIDER SCROLLS

The wider the scroll surrounding a floral pattern, the more shades are necessary to do it justice. It is the combination of tones that add beauty to the scroll, rather than a wide expanse of one shade by itself. In other words, the color series when hooked should afford a pleasing blended effect, with no one shade predominating. These wider scrolls may use anywhere from four to seven shades or even more of a single color, hooked in single rows, or fingered in as in oversize leaf scrolls, and equally graded from light to dark. Outline the scroll first with the lightest shade and do the remaining shades after veining.

VEINS IN SCROLLS

If the scroll is of sufficient width to use more than three shades of a color, a vein of contrasting color can be very effective. When used, veining lines should be very much apparent after the scroll is hooked. Sometimes a slightly wider cutting of strip is advantageous, especially if the material is thin. If using very fine woolen, you may need to hook two rows in the widest part of the vein.

Veins should always be done after the outline and before filling in with the remaining shades. They are designed and hooked in much the same fashion as leaf veining and may run down the center of the scroll, following its contours. Veining is used most often in scroll patterns that closely resemble leaves, or are actually designed from leaf forms, but the use of it is entirely optional.

VEINS OF PLAIDS OR OTHER MIXTURES

While veins are most frequently hooked in a dark shade, plaids or other gay mixtures can be equally attractive in many designs. These colorful mixtures lose their identity completely when hooked in the scroll, but add a wonderful sparkle to the design. Scotch plaids containing reds, greens, yellows, blues, etc., are lovely as veining in just about any colored scroll. It is usually possible, as well as desirable, to find a plaid or other mixture which includes the scroll color, in addition to its other various combinations. Yet it is the plaid's contrasting shades that will add the most glamor to your scroll in a narrow band of veining.

Checks can also be used to good advantage, but will afford less contrast. Checks of black and white or brown and white, tinted in the scroll color, work well, the latter combination being especially attractive in a gold or tan scroll.

DOUBLE SCROLL IN ONE UNIT

Double scrolls can be designed attractively with a two-tone combination. When the separate division is apparent in the design, it is pleasing to have the major part of the unit in one color (or a color series), such as green or blue, matching a color in the center of the rug, and the adjoining

Fig. 64. A two-toned scroll. Suggested color scheme: X, red Scotch plaid tinted in golden yellow dye; 1, light green; 2, medium green; 3, dark green; 4, light golden yellow; 5, medium golden yellow; 6, dark golden yellow.

part or the twin scroll in soft golds. When doing this type of scroll, a mixture or gay plaid still may be used as veining. Whatever material you finally select for this purpose, be sure to include the same veining in each of the twin scrolls, so that colors are properly related. This more elaborate type of scroll is better suited to larger rugs and may add greatly to the charm of the final result. A word of caution, however. In the case of the two-tone scroll, it is wise to use muted colorings, since contrast is already afforded by the two-color combination.

BORDERS AFFECT YOUR SCROLL SHADING

If the border of a rug is to be dark, then a light outline for the scroll is best. If, on the other hand, it is to be light, be sure that the scroll edge is of sufficient depth for a pleasant contrast. The same principle applies to

(Photo: Vern Hamilton)

Roses and Buds, 40 by 64 inches, hooked by Clara Spencer. A very light blue background, gold scroll, and dark blue border provide a striking setting for the roses, which range from deep red in the center to pink into red in the corners.

Seven Iris rug, 40 by 68 inches, designed by Beth Lucas and hooked by Leah Brown. The fernlike scroll is merely outlined, with a single line of blue-green. Natural flower colors are muted against soft pink at center which deepens toward scroll. Border is a rich mahogany color.

backgrounds, so study the arrangement of your colors carefully before you start hooking, and make any adaptations that seem necessary in the order of your scroll colors.

CHOOSING SCROLL COLOR

Although all rules seem to be made to be broken—and often with attractive results—we must at least observe them until we are experienced hookers or experienced designers and know exactly what results we are going to get in color combinations. For instance, the golden rule is never to use cool shades such as blue and green together (a blue scroll and green border for your rug, for instance) nor should we mix warm colors such as rust and wine. Blues or greens separately are excellent near rose or gold tones and any color will go with white, gray, or black. A never-ending source of attractive color combinations will be found in printed materials, wallpapers, and illustrations in magazines or books. It is always worth noting the proportions of different colors that a decorator combines in a room. There are usually three shades, one predominating, with a second contrasting, and a third harmonizing. For example, if a cool tone of green or blue predominates, warm tones of red may be chosen to give contrast, and gold, beige, or gray might act as a harmonizing color.

COLOR SUGGESTIONS

Scroll	Background	Border
Gold	Cream, beige, gray, or black	Blue, green, wine, brown, or black
Dusty rose	Neutral light	Blue, green, gray, or brown
Blue	Neutral light	Rose, gold, gray, or cocoa
Green	Neutral light	Rose, gold, darker green, brown, or gray

Use any color scroll with a black or brown rug, but choose light tones for proper contrast with dark coloring.

Victorian scroll pattern.

19
HOW IS YOUR BACKGROUND?

When reference is made to the background of a rug this means the space between the central floral grouping and the scroll or border, also any leftover space among the floral grouping. If there is no center grouping, the background is the entire space within the scroll or border of the rug. In the block or geometric pattern, the background is the space surrounding the design and all the way to the edge of the rug.

When planning a background color, consider among other things the use of the rug, and where it is to be placed. A rug destined to bear much traffic, or to be in a relatively dark corner of an entry hall, perhaps, can well stand the use of strong coloring, whereas one designed for the average bedroom would be more suitable with a light neutral-colored background.

NEUTRAL SHADES

Beige, light or dark tans, grays, cocoa shades or ecrus always look well in backgrounds. While these colors are anything but a new idea, the selection of one of them is never unwise for it will flatter the coloring of any pattern. A neutral-colored background also provides the opportunity of using a strong color in the scroll or border when desired. In other words, these shades act as useful blenders when colorful patterns are used. They are always a safe choice.

ANTIQUE WHITE BACKGROUND

White mellowed down to look old is usually referred to as antique white. (See dyeing instructions in chapter 14.) It looks much better in the background of a rug than pure white, and is more practical for long wear. Because of its mellowed coloring, antique white does wonderful things for the old-fashioned nosegay patterns, enhancing the gaily colored flowers in a way that no other background color ever quite equals. Often this white is used for both background and border. As with any light color used in large areas, antique white should be featured in rugs not earmarked for heavy traffic.

PASTELS FOR BACKGROUNDS

Choosing a pastel shade is more or less a new idea for a rug background, but it can be very flattering indeed. Care must be exercised to select just the right shade, for unless it is very soft and subdued the whole effect of the rug will suffer. Success lies in choosing a tint rather than a color, whether it be of green, blue, pink, or another shade. Pastel tints are particularly successful in backgrounds when the borders are worked in a darker material of the same color. In this case, the scroll color must be carefully planned, too, making sure to have a soft shading either in a cool or warm color, whichever will contrast harmoniously with the background and border. A charming color scheme, for instance, is a blue border with a lighter blue background and a scroll in dusty rose, especially if the rug features pink roses in the center grouping. Rugs done in soft greens with gold scrolls are equally attractive, and there are many other combinations that you will find suited to your requirements. Brown or black borders can also be used with beige, antique white, and pastel backgrounds.

BLACK OR BROWN BACKGROUNDS

These were chosen by our grandmothers and great-grandmothers because they were so practical. For the same reason, they are just as popular today. No color emphasizes gay colorings of a center nosegay more strongly than black, which may be the reason why men especially favor this type of rug. Black backgrounds go especially well in rooms with a Victorian atmosphere—always demanding a great deal of attention. Hasn't it been said that "Grandma's cabbage roses blinked when you looked at them"? No doubt a black background had a great deal to do with the illusion.

Brown backgrounds and borders are less dramatic than black yet offer greater richness than most other colors. Many hookers choose brown as a very practical blender. It will modestly accentuate the beauty of all flower colors, will not show dirt as easily as lighter hues, or dust as easily as large expanses of black.

COLORS NOT SUITABLE AS BACKGROUNDS

Never use a very bright or garish color for your background, as this almost invariably cheapens the appearance of the rug. Once departing from the tans, beiges, grays, pastels, antique whites, or very dark colors, the chances are practically nil for an attractive rug unless the in-between shades are muted. For instance, a dark rose may be exquisite with a border in the brown-wine coloring, providing the rose has a dusty rose cast. This goes for blue too, which, if in a medium tone (neither pastel nor dark) should be dyed with gray to a more subdued blue. A medium gray-blue background would be lovely with a dark blue border.

The muting of bright or dark color with gray, brown, or other dye can make stronger backgrounds effective when such are called for by the furnishings of a room. If using a more intense color for a background, be sure to use either the same coloring or a darker one for the border, so the two are related. Imagine, for instance, a multicolored floral nosegay competing with an Alice blue, jade green, or scarlet background—the rug would jump at you every time you came into the room. Golds, if not overbright, are sometimes chosen, though even this color range may detract from a center arrangement unless planned very carefully. However, in-between colors can always be grayed down or softened by dyeing, should you have a lot of bright colors on hand that you want to use up. The old saying "the stronger the color, the less of it to use" certainly applies to hooked rugs—in the bright shades, at least.

SHADOWING AMONG THE FLOWERS

Though many hookers find it pleasing to feature a shadow in the background of their floral groupings, this is purely a matter of personal choice. When using beige, tan, gray, or other neutral coloring, a slightly darker shade of the same (or nearly the same) color can be used effectively for filling in among the flowers and leaves. When shadowing among the floral grouping, it is best to continue it in one, or no more than two, outlines around the outside of the floral grouping. Allow such outlines to follow the contour of each flower and leaf exactly before filling in the remaining background. Even though the shadowing idea began with the use of tan, beige, or other neutral coloring, a new trend is toward shadowing in stronger colors. For example, if you are using the dusty rose background with a dark brownish-wine border—mentioned before—the results are enhanced if you use your dark border color as shadowing for the central part of the background within the floral grouping. However, plan this center shadowing so it changes from the dark to a *slightly* lighter coloring, as it nears the edge of the centerpiece; working this way there will be no sudden jump from the wine shadowing into the rose background. If done correctly, subtle shadowing of this nature creates such a smooth and pleasing overall blending that upon first glance at the rug no one is aware that shadowing has been used at all. Remember that the perfect test of good blending in a rug is when no one part hits you in the eye upon first glance.

When hooking the shadowed area of a centerpiece make one, or perhaps two, rows of the darker color to outline the individual flowers and leaves, then fill in. The shadowy effect produced between the design and the remaining background gives greater emphasis to your flowers. The tone of the shadow should, of course, be in harmony with that of the background, being from one to three shades darker. For antique-white or pastel-shade backgrounds no shadowing need be used among the floral grouping. The black or brown rug, too, should have the entire background in the same color.

MATERIALS FOR BACKGROUNDS AND BORDERS

Coats with a furry texture and not too thick work best in backgrounds and borders, such spacing requiring a considerable amount of material. One coat of full length in a lady's size would be about right for the background of a 3-by-5-foot rug, and the border requiring about the same amount. Another advantage here is that it is usually possible to accumulate old coats of neutral or dark shades without too much effort, thus avoiding the necessity of dyeing. Old blankets, yellowed by age, may be just right for an antique-white background, and woolen skirts or slacks may also be blended in these larger spaces.

HIT-OR-MISS BACKGROUNDS

In block patterns containing flowers, it is usually best to fill in the entire block with a neutral-colored background such as a tan, beige, brown, gray, or black. Very dark shades of green, navy blue, or other deep colors are also suitable on occasion. If the rug pattern varies with alternate plain blocks made hit-or-miss fashion (in lines of varied lengths), or in the half-circle method described later on, these blocks can be very attractive hooked in various tans, shepherd checks, or brown-and-tan plaid mixtures. A half-dozen harmonizing shades in this color range could be mixed in together to complete a larger rug, a hall runner, or stair carpet—in fact, wherever more material is required than any one garment will provide. The brown or tan mixtures are but one example—any other color could be featured in different materials and patterns.

An assortment of gay colors along with beiges and browns looks lovely in hit-or-miss block designs without floral centers. Bright red combined with neutral shades is gay and old-fashioned. Brown, green, and yellow along with the tans is a good choice, too, especially if the rug is to be used with pine and maple. In the hit-or-miss rug, informality is always in order.

20

FILLING IN BACKGROUNDS AND BORDERS AND ADDITIONAL BORDER IDEAS

Although it is always permissible to fill in backgrounds and borders in straight rows across the width of the rug, this procedure is usually dropped once the craftsman has developed the knack of easy hooking. To do the first rug in this manner, however, develops good hooking technique, and is excellent practice for learning to pull through even loops. It is also particularly effective in certain types of rugs such as the one described next.

THE ALL-BLACK VICTORIAN RUG

The Victorian rug with its center nosegay and colorful scroll is charmingly old-fashioned when its background is done in straight rows across the width. This manner of filling in gives it all the attractiveness of a fine piece of petit point, and it is delightfully different from the usual hooked rug.

GEOMETRICS AND BLOCK DESIGNS

Hit-or-miss designs are usually hooked in rows across each block. For these, at least three or four materials in the required color range work out to better advantage. The idea is to use strips of perhaps 15 to 18 inches from each piece of material, hooking one strip from one piece, then a strip from another, etc., filling in the background from right to left. Strips will end at various places, and the changing from one material to another

(Photo: Max Tatch)

An Early American Victorian rug with an all-black background hooked by the author. Typical are the cabbage roses and elaborate scroll in green.

creates the hit-or-miss background. Different shades of plain-colored material, checks, plaids, or tweeds in related coloring can be used. Various tans are especially good.

When the blocks are broken up in odd shapes, resembling checkerboards or old-fashioned quilts, etc., they fall into the geometric classification. For these designs various contrasting colors may be assembled to form the patterned effects. Here you are at liberty to combine bright and subdued colors to suit your fancy, taking your cue from old-fashioned quilts, such as the Flower Garden, the Wedding Ring, Crazy Quilt, and others. Study these charming old quilts at neighbors' houses, at museums, in magazine reproductions, or wherever possible, and you will get many ideas for unusual patterns and colors. Books on quilts offer a wealth of ideas both for designing and color.

WAVY-LINE BACKGROUNDS

Many hookers start filling in by spacing wavy lines all over the background, scattering them here and there and letting them extend in various directions. Then, with the burlap tension somewhat equalized, it is just a matter of filling in following the various established lines. One material could be used to make the first wavy lines, with another material of a similar shade filling in the adjoining space. By alternating in this manner, materials can be blended as one, making a variegated background. Even when one material or two very similar materials are used in this way, a slight design will still be seen in the pattern, softening the background and adding to the general attractiveness of the rug. A word of warning, however: There should be comparatively little variation in the shading of the background, since a very marked variation in colored materials would detract too much from the floral center.

THE HALF-CIRCLE BACKGROUND

The author's favorite background is made by the half-circle method. By using this device for filling in, as many as six different materials can be used—and when these are evenly blended the background can look as if it were hooked from a single material.

Begin by hooking little half circles (about 2 inches in length), scattering them all over the background as demonstrated in fig. 65. These half circles, arranged in no particular set way, can lie in each and every direction, interlocking, overlapping, underlapping—however you like.

The second step is to overline each half circle, connecting lines as you go. (If you are blending two materials, the other is used for the second step.) In other words, instead of stopping at the end of the half circle, the curved line continues until reaching the line of a neighboring half circle.

Fig. 65. A half-circle pattern can be used for hooking the background instead of straight rows.

Having reached a stopping point, the row is ended by cutting the strip at that spot, and starting again, this time, perhaps underlining each half circle (if you are working with a third material, use it now for underlining), and connecting lines as before. When more than one material is being used for the background, vary each set of lines in the same way as you proceed so the materials are evenly distributed and well blended, as described in detail shortly. In this manner, the entire background is filled, resulting in an attractive textural pattern.

MIXING MATERIALS IN BACKGROUNDS AND BORDERS

In the first place, try to combine materials that are very much alike in coloring so they will blend well when hooked in neighboring curved lines. This is particularly necessary around a floral nosegay. With too much contrast in your background mixture a confused, restless feeling will result, and the full beauty of your floral grouping will be lost. Better to use a plain or nearly plain material for any background surrounding a center grouping. Never consider the use of a plaid mixture unless it is a muted blending with very slight variation, as occasionally found in beiges or grays. Brown and beige mixtures or black and white dyed over is recommended for the border, insofar as mixtures are concerned.

When filling in a background with half circles (fig. 65), choose one material to make each of the half circles, a second to overline, and a third material to underline them. A fourth material can be used to fill in all

133

remaining space. In this manner the background of a room-size rug, 7 by 9 feet, can be filled in with four full-length ladies' coats, the border requiring an additional amount equal to that of the background. Four coats are equivalent to about 10 yards of 54-inch material or perhaps 10 pounds of woolen.. (This allows a generous amount as it is always best to have material left rather than run short.) The background estimate includes shadowing for the floral grouping too. It is not too difficult to pick up old coats—moth-eaten, stained, or outmoded—and by procuring eight of them from thrift shops, rummage sales, or friends, you will be sure to have enough for a large rug without worry of running out of material .

MIXTURES FOR BORDERS

When discussing scrolls and backgrounds in other chapters, we also, of necessity, brought up the question of border colors, for all of these design features are closely related. We should, however, spend a little more time on the question of mixed borders using checks, plaids, and other such materials, for a variegated border can be enchanting.

The use of checks and plaids in a border is particularly suitable when a rug has a floral center and a scroll. Backgrounds made in shades of beige generally look best with a mixed border of browns, while the scroll can be of any color flattering to these colors or in a very much lighter or darker shade of beige or brown—just so long as there is enough contrast. Earlier in the book it was suggested that the scroll, when used, gave the opportunity to repeat a color used in the central grouping of flowers and foliage. Thus on a mixed brown border a restful green might be introduced in the scroll for a lively contrasting effect. Pastel backgrounds in blue, green, or rose are beautifully framed in navy, dark green, or wine, respectively, with a light, neutral-colored scroll, such as the cocoa shades, beiges into darker tans, or light into darker grays. Undyed brown plaids, checks, or other mixtures of this type intermingled, will result in softer tones than a border hooked in a solid color. Or brown and white checks or other such mixtures tinted with a little beige to soften the coloring may be preferred. Not only do such combinations in a border make an interesting texture, but they are restful, flattering to the center pattern, and practical for wear. Whatever material you select for the mixed border, be sure the predominating color of each is approximately the same.

A black and white check (or any other dark color with white) makes a strong and handsome border for rugs which feature these colors elsewhere. A particularly interesting effect can also be obtained by tinting a black and white check green. The author used this most successfully in a rug with a soft dusty-rose scroll and a light beige background.

The above are only a few suggestions out of countless possibilities. As in every craft, it is up to the individual to experiment and develop his or her preferences, adapting the material most readily at hand.

DARK BORDERS

In the old days very dark borders such as black, dark brown, or green were the most popular, framing the rugs in much the same manner as the heavy and ornate frames enclosed the pictures. Dark borders are always flattering to flowered centers and are still a suitable choice for Victorian-style rooms. Even in modern rug designs for contemporary interiors, the dark border finds its place.

DON'T USE VIVID BORDERS

Vivid, sharp colors, if included at all in a rug, are for highlights and accents and should be used in moderation. For this reason, they are not suitable for the comparatively large area of a border. Occasionally there may be exceptions such as a rug for a very dark corner of a passageway where the brightness is toned down, or for a child's room, or for some very special planned effect in a modern room, but generally speaking keep to more subdued colors. Even a rose shade is preferable if it has a dusty rose cast and green is prettier in a misty shade of reseda or a gray-green. The same goes for blue. In principle, never use a tone that jumps when you look at the rug, and never let it be brighter than the colors used in the rest of the design.

BEIGE, TANS, PASTELS FOR BORDERS

When in harmony with the scroll, any of these shades may be used, but they should either match or be darker than the background. Never choose a border color that is lighter than the background.

21
ADDITIONAL HINTS ON HOOKING

LIGHT

Some people are more comfortable with one type and strength of light than another while hooking, but the main thing is to have sufficient light to do good work without straining your eyes. Sit as near a window as possible. Hooking is probably one of the easiest handicrafts on the eyes there is, but light is essential for good blending of colors. Electric light is fine if it is directly over one's work.

TAKE TIME OFF

Sit in a straight-back chair and try not to slump over your work. When you find yourself stooping over, take time out to sit erect. By forming this habit you won't feel overtired after a long spell of hooking. It's also a good idea to stop hooking occasionally and exercise your neck. Relax your muscles by turning your head sideways as far as you can in each direction. Hooking is such an absorbing occupation that one is apt to forget to take care of one's body while working for hours on end. Your hooking will be all the better for a little time off occasionally.

136

STUDY YOUR WORK BETWEEN OTHER JOBS

Each time you finish hooking, it's an excellent idea to hang the frame in a convenient place where you can cast an occasional glance at your work while you set about your routine housework or other jobs. The author has a favorite spot in her kitchen, where in-between times, her current work is always hung on a nail for critical observation. Studying your work in this manner and at an appropriate distance enables you to judge the rug as a whole as it progresses. With a fresh eye constantly going over your work, you will see what needs to be done next, where a touch more color might improve the design, perhaps, whether you will put in one more flower or leaf, or else leave some other detail out which you had originally planned to put in. Seeing your rug in a new perspective, you are able to look at it more objectively than when occupied with small areas while actually hooking.

YOU DON'T HAVE TO BE A PERFECTIONIST

Remember, no handwork of this nature is supposed to be perfect in each and every detail. That is the great charm of hooked rugs. They should always have a handmade look. Leave mechanical perfection to machines. Many beginners are apt to become overtense and critical of their work, especially after laboring on a rug for some time. The old saying "so close to the trees that they can't see the forest" exactly describes the way some ruggers view their work. In the author's beginners' classes she has seen many a hooker do perfectly satisfactory work yet refuse to appreciate the overall effect because of some minute flaw that is visible to him or her only. Modesty is an admirable quality, but sometimes it can be carried too far. Hooking a rug is to be enjoyed in all its phases, so don't be despondent over minor deviations, for nine times out of ten they will not show up to disadvantage in the final result.

SAVE TIME WHEN HOOKING FLOWERS AND LEAVES

As soon as you start hooking flowers and leaves, get into the habit of fastening together each series of colors in individual groups. Use a safety pin, clothes pin, or sew a thread through each grouping, with shades arranged in proper order from light to dark. When using a particular series, you can then progress from one shade to the next without unintentionally omitting any one of them. You will also save much time otherwise spent in searching through a random assortment of colors.

When you are through using one color series, just roll up the set of pinned strips and neatly put them aside before starting on another. In this way your materials will never become mixed and create unnecessary

Fig. 66. A safety pin makes a handy support for scissors while working.

confusion. By keeping your materials neat and orderly, you will enjoy your hobby all the more.

KEEP YOUR WORK PLACE IN ORDER

Some people get so carried away by their work that they forget their surroundings completely. This often results in a room that looks as if a whirlwind had swept through it. Whether you have a hobby room or not, it is a good idea to retain at least a certain semblance of order so that you can do your best work and don't have a major cleaning up operation at the end of a day. A small pasteboard box and a whisk broom for occasionally brushing off the rug pattern are necessities for most hookers' peace of mind. Keep these handy. Place different-colored materials in different boxes and label them so you don't have to go rummaging through a pile of assorted colors for the ones you need. Have a wastepaper basket nearby when cutting strips, so that odd ends, fluff, and lint don't scatter all over the floor. Sweep up the floor every time you leave your work. Keep your tools—rug hooks, scissors, extra thumbtacks, etc.—together in a small box so they don't get lost in between times or swept up with any debris. Keep neat files or scrapbooks of illustrations that you may be using as inspirational material so you will know just where to find what you are looking for. All these suggestions, and others you will think of for yourself, will help to keep an orderly room which in turn will evoke better work.

A HANDY PLACE TO KEEP SCISSORS WHILE HOOKING

A safety pin large enough to prevent your scissors from falling or sliding off your rug as you are hooking is a great convenience. Pin this horizontally with the pattern and within easy reach on the right-hand side. While not in use, your scissors may be slipped in the pin as shown in fig. 66.

138

22

WHY NOT MAKE YOUR OWN PATTERN?

If not immediately, the time will come sooner or later when you will want to design your own rug pattern. Then you can be as original as you like. By developing a keen sense of observation, you will find many worth-while ideas for patterns everywhere you look. You may want to copy old patterns, borrow from folk designs, adapt illustrations, or find your inspirations in wallpapers, floral chintzes, and other drapery materials, or directly in nature itself.

Whether your design is based on any of the above suggestions or the other ideas discussed in this book, you will find that vellum paper is your best friend. Transparent vellum paper comes in widths from 18 to 48 inches, and is sold by the yard, or in parcels of 5 or 6 yards, at most stationery stores.

TRACING OTHER PATTERNS

If you plan to copy the outline and shading of one or more flowers or leaves in a printed fabric, lay a piece of vellum paper directly over the material and trace the outlines with a lead pencil. Do the same with wallpaper, needlepoint, seed catalogs, or any other printed design you plan to use. In this manner, various flowers may be assembled on numerous pieces of paper before you start the actual design of your rug pattern.

WORKING OUT YOUR OWN DESIGN

Work out your rug design on a large, rug-size piece of vellum paper first, before transferring it to burlap. The easiest method is to arrange your separate tracings of flowers, leaves, or other objects on a table or the floor, grouping them in the arrangement you like best. Larger blossoms should be nearest the center, with smaller ones more or less evenly distributed around them as described in chapter 23. Arrange and rearrange the tracings until you are satisfied with the general effect, then lay your rug-size vellum over the grouping and trace the entire arrangement. Even after you have made this tracing, changes may be made here and there up to the time you actually transfer the pattern onto burlap. The completed design is transferred to burlap by means of carbon paper and a blunt pencil for tracing as described shortly, after which the pattern may be inked with regular ink using an ordinary pen. It is important that the vellum paper design be securely pinned to the burlap, at one end at least, while tracing is being done so that no movement is permitted.

In making up your own design, it is of course important to know what effect you are striving for, so that the selection of individual flowers and their coloring can be made intelligently before you start your tracings. It's a good idea to make a small, rough sketch of the type of arrangement you want and adapt this later wherever necessary as you arrange your tracings into the finished pattern. How to enlarge or reduce patterns so they are the correct size for your rug is described in chapter 23.

WHAT BURLAP TO USE

A medium-weight burlap of natural color is the ideal rug foundation. This is a twelve- or fourteen-ounce burlap. Though usable, a ten-ounce burlap is rather flimsy and loose, while a sixteen-ounce material is somewhat heavy for satisfactory work, threads being likely to break as work progresses.

Monk's cloth in both single and double ply is widely used instead of burlap for a rug foundation, some people preferring this material. There is also a warp cloth available that is very good for rug hooking, though it is possibly more costly. Regular needlepoint canvas is also usable, though expensive.

PREPARING BURLAP FOR DESIGN

Before attempting to transfer a design from vellum paper onto burlap, cut the burlap to the desired size. Allow at least a 2½-inch margin outside the limits of your pattern, then pull a thread across the ends to make sure of straight edges, and hem. Next establish the correct border lines, i.e., the limits of the area to be hooked. Before pinning on the vellum pattern, mark the exact center of burlap, for correct placement of the design. This center point is necessary whether doing a pattern that is centered on a rug or one that has an off-center balance as some modern designs feature.

JOINING BURLAP FOR A ROOM-SIZE RUG

Sometimes it is necessary to join together two or more pieces of burlap for a large rug. Overlap selvage edges ¼ to ⅜ of an inch, and sew by machine along each edge, as near to the selvage as possible. First sew one side of the burlap, then turn it over and sew down the overlapping edge on the other side. This seam will make no difference in the appearance of the rug when it is hooked. When hooking through a double seam, first punch holes with a punch or other sharp instrument as each loop is hooked, so materials will not break as they are pulled through this tight area. Always hook across the seam instead of lengthwise, since this is easier and also strengthens the joining.

TRANSFERRING DESIGNS ONTO BURLAP

Patience is required when transferring the design onto burlap, as some carbon papers will result in clear lines, while others require repeated drawing for sufficient clarity. Never remove the vellum drawing until the outlines of the pattern are obvious on the burlap. The carbon lines don't necessarily have to be strong, as faint lines may be picked up when the pattern is gone over with pen and ink. When you are ready to ink in the pattern, you will find that the carbon drawing will show more clearly if you sit in a shadowed light. While it may be possible to do a small pattern without inking, it is generally best to strengthen the lines in this manner since carbon rubs off as the pattern is handled, losing much of the detail.

Though it takes some effort to make your own pattern, more patience than skill is required, and it is a most satisfactory feeling to know that the rug is your own creation from start to finish.

THE SHAPE OF YOUR RUGS

It is best to stick to rectangular, square, oval, or round rugs, rather than to attempt scalloped, triangular, or other fancy shapes which are seldom in good taste and are not nearly so practical. The proportions of 2 by 4, 3 by 5, 4 by 6, or 5 by 7½ feet are always a safe choice for rectangular and oval rugs. Round or square rugs, particularly, should be designed for specific settings as they are less adaptable to a change of locale.

23

DIFFERENT TYPES OF DESIGNS

Although the floral pattern is unquestionably the most popular type of design with most hookers, and can be designed to suit almost any type of room, there is no reason at all why quite different types of designs should not be selected. Some contemporary furnishings may call for a modern adaptation of the floral motif such as shown in fig. 67, while other all-modern rooms may depart entirely from the traditional as shown in fig. 71. Modern paintings might readily prove the inspiration for many such designs, particularly abstract designs based on geometrical forms. Old Colonial houses with wide floor boards and low ceilings may look best with the Early American patterns and original designs based on folk art motifs.

Still other designs may be required for a child's room, for instance, where a pattern based on an animal design might be worked out as shown in figs. 76 and 77.

MODERN DESIGNS

For modern florals, a large and simple design is recommended. Bold forms without fussy details are usually featured, and the design is often placed off center. You might start your design from one corner, allowing the main flower to occupy half of the rug and balance this with smaller stylized details. The following flowers of large proportions are particularly appropriate: poppy, magnolia blossom, rose, lily, morning glory, daisy, any

Fig. 67. Calla lily pattern in a modern grouping.

Fig. 68. A conventional centerpiece can also be hooked in a rug without scroll or border.

large, open-petal flower—or perhaps just leaves, sometimes of the tropical variety. Oak leaves or ferns make a very good choice.

Even the over-sized block pattern, with a large single flower in every other plain block, is as suitable for the modern room as it is for traditional furnishings. Another suggestion for the modern design may be a wide diagonal band running from opposite corners, with a scattered grouping of perhaps three or four flowers featured across the band.

Fig. 69. A modern rug design with an ancient heraldic rose in the center.

Modern designs are more characteristic, however, when the patterns are more abstract and when flowers, if used at all, are more of a heraldic nature such as the rose in fig. 69.

Another stylized pattern is shown in the rug illustrated on page 146. This rug was hooked following the instructions in this book when still in manuscript form.

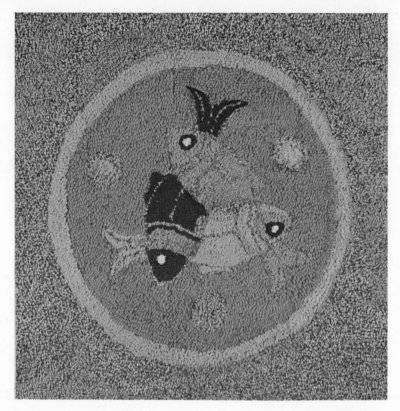

(Photo: Criterion Photocraft)

Three Fishes. A modern rug with central motif enlarged from design at left. The fishes are black, red, and golden yellow on a blue center circled in red. Bubbles and background are hooked in gray tweed. The rug was made by Joseph Slater.

Star Compass. Another modern design, hooked by Joseph Slater. Circle in center is of muted grass green. Pointers are in black alternated by shorter ones in rust red, small diamond pointers are golden yellow. The border is edged in black with red and green inner circles.

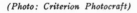

(Photo: Criterion Photocraft)

Fig. 70. Another simple compass design for a hallway rug.

The ultra-modern room features the simplest of lines and large areas of plain colors. Rugs should conform to this general plan, and it is not difficult to design plain patterns. A rug can be all one color; it can be designed checkerboard fashion or in diamond blocks; it can be plain with a large colored star in the center and a border of small stars around the edge; it can be composed of colored bands with an effect somewhat similar to a braided rug; it can be abstract like a modern painting, composed of triangles and circles. The combinations of simple forms are endless.

EARLY AMERICAN DESIGNS

Perhaps one of the most popular Early American designs is the small block pattern, with blocks of perhaps 8 or 10 inches square. These may be planned to be hooked hit-or-miss fashion throughout, the hooked lines in each block running in the opposite direction to the neighboring one. See fig. 72. Another idea might be to have the blocks hexagon or diamond

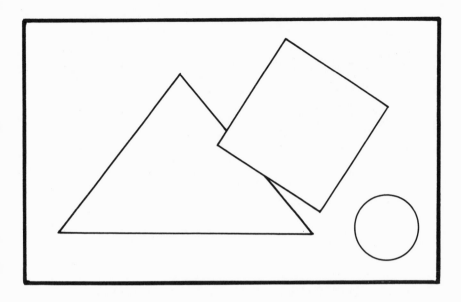

Fig. 71. Abstract design. Square, triangle, circle, and background could be hooked in different harmonizing colors to match any specific decor.

Fig. 72. Plain block pattern. Squares are hooked alternately in horizontal and vertical rows. Color variation can be brown or gray in the vertical lines, multicolored rows in horizontal lines.

Fig. 73. A smaller block pattern can be hooked in variegated colors.

shape as in fig. 74. By varying the color, also the direction of hooking in each adjoining block, a pattern of alternating colors is worked out. A multicolored rug could also be planned with this design in harlequin fashion. Alternate blocks could be in beige or another neutral shade, while the ones in between could be in a gay mixture of odd colors, in hit-or-miss lines. Yet another variation would be to break up the background in each alter-

Fig. 74. Diamond block pattern. Hook diamonds in alternating rows. Center row (lengthwise), also top and bottom half diamonds, might be worked in neutral color such as beige, tan, or gray, while remaining two rows of diamonds could feature a bright color or mixture for a harlequin effect.

150

nate block, hooking small irregular patches of various colors, such as in a patchwork quilt. The block pattern can be designed to go equally well in an old or modern setting.

GEOMETRIC DESIGNS

Though geometric designs have been suggested as motifs for modern rugs, these shapes were frequently included in informal rugs of earlier days. The chief difference, perhaps, between an early geometric rug and one of modern design lies in the arrangement. The traditional rug was designed

Fig. 75. Mosaic block pattern. The mosaic squares are made up of irregular shapes or patches of different harmonious colors. Alternate squares should be in a neutral color.

with a scattering of different shapes or a very symmetrical arrangement of circles and squares, while the modern rug is very carefully planned with a perfectly balanced asymmetrical arrangement of much larger squares, triangles, circles, or lines—as in a modern painting. Quilts or quilt patterns offer many ideas for the early geometric arrangements. A pattern with squares might be divided up with circles or semicircles made by placing a plate or saucer in each block, and tracing around it, thus achieving geometric blocks to suit your fancy.

151

For a modern geometric or abstract pattern, study the more sophisticated magazines, art magazines, or go to an exhibition of abstract paintings in a city museum or gallery, where you should get many ideas for forms and colors.

PRIMITIVE DESIGNS

These may be rough drawings of almost any subjects. The early folk painters or itinerant artists of America were not trained as professionals and their work, which we see today in museums and private collections, has a characteristic naive charm that endears it to us all. The entirely realistic picture is not suited to rug hooking, and that is why amateurs can, in primitive fashion, make their own renderings of any such subject as a dog, cat, or bowl of fruit with excellent results. This type of rug is best suited to the nursery, playroom, or perhaps the hallway. Primitive designs can also look charming on a stair carpet as shown in the color plate on page 157. Rugs of this nature are best kept small; 2 by 4 feet is a good size. Of course, the exception is the stair carpet, but even in this case each scene is kept within the small area provided by each step of the staircase.

By looking at early American folk paintings or studying reproductions of them in magazines or books, you will soon get an idea of what you might do. Nor is this the only source. One lady recently used her child's drawings for a primitive block design, which ran as follows: her child's version of a train ran across the top blocks, railroad, smoke and all, just as the child had scrawled it. The lower blocks featured the hand of the child in one block, a teddy bear in another, his playmates in two others, and so on. Children's drawings are full of life and imagination. They know how to draw free hand and their efforts, being unself-conscious, often represent true primitive design. We can therefore take a lesson from them sometimes.

Try your hand at some very simple design. Don't make it elaborate and don't try for perfection. You might like to work out a rural scene, such as a red barn surrounded by a pasture with cows grazing, or some other farm scene.

Primitive designs also fit the modern interior, especially if you get your inspiration from the art of primitive peoples, such as those living in Africa, New Guinea, or some of the Pacific islands. A single primitive symbolic figure could occupy the center of an otherwise plain rug, with much the same effect as a modern painting.

HOW TO ENLARGE A DESIGN (fig. 76)

To double the size of any picture you may have sketched or traced on vellum paper, first mark off the picture into 1-inch squares. Then on an-

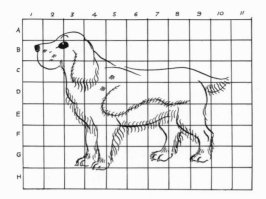

Original tracing

Enlargement

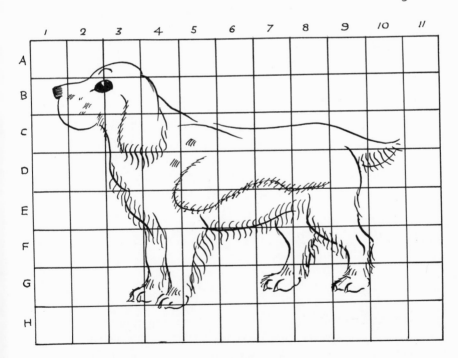

Fig. 76. Any desired pattern copied or traced from a print or other illustration can be enlarged as shown. Rule up even squares over original tracing on vellum paper, then mark up same number of squares on larger sheet and copy pattern section by section within each square.

other piece of vellum, rule up the outer dimensions of your picture, doubling its length and breath. Next, divide the large piece of vellum into 2-inch squares exactly corresponding to the 1-inch squares on the smaller sheet. Now it is just a matter of making line drawings in the 2-inch squares to match the drawings in the 1-inch squares. By doing just one square at a time, you will be surprised how easy it is. And even if a few inaccuracies occur, this does not matter in the primitive design.

HOOKING THE PRIMITIVE DESIGN

It is unnecessary to have much, if any, special shading in the primitive design. Solid colors are used extensively instead of a color series. One color may serve the purpose for doing a particular subject—a house, for instance, with black or any other dark outline to delineate windows, doors, shutters, etc. This does not mean that you should not put in a shadowed wall in a darker color if you want to, or green shutters on either side of the window—this depends entirely on the inclinations of each hooker. There are no set rules.

The actual hooking process remains the same as with any other type of rug, except that hooking may be coarser with wider cutting of strips if you like. A certain amount of unevenness of hooking is of no concern in the average primitive design.

NURSERY DESIGNS

Rabbits, kittens, or the three bears are popular subjects for the child's room. Designs to copy or trace and enlarge (as described earlier) are, of course, to be found in juvenile classics on the child's own bookshelf. Realistic touches when hooking an animal design may be obtained by using furry angora woolen materials in white.

A sailboat design might be appropriate for a boy's rug. It's easy and fun to hook and the subject provides the opportunity of action—always popular with young fry. Books, magazines, catalogs may provide you with a picture of this nature to copy or trace.

ORIENTAL DESIGNS

These can be copied from the rugs themselves or from museum reproductions in catalogs or on colored cards. It takes a lot of patience to work such patterns out, since there is so much minute detail. Simplified adaptations are advisable, as it is not possible, of course, to duplicate the fine weave of a loom. Many motifs can be borrowed, however, and excellent results have been achieved in hooked rugs inspired by classic oriental designs. You may do best with this kind of rug using yarn and the hollow-handle hook.

Fig. 77. Three animal patterns. The stag and hen are realistic, the third is a typical stylized folk design.

Folk Dancers. A colorful rug designed and hooked by Ellen C. Gould.

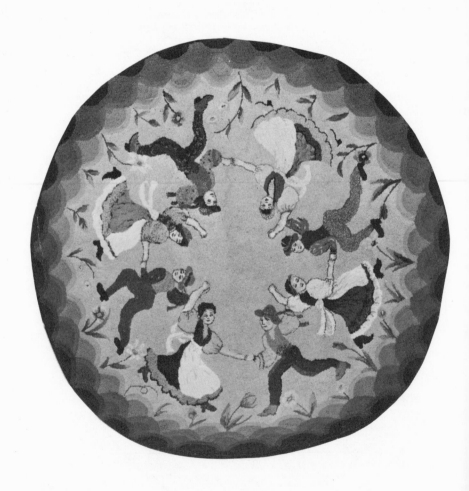

(Photo: John W. Wilson)

Harvest Fruit, by the author. This colorful chair seat glows with rich colors and subtle shading.

(Photo: George de Gennaro, courtesy "Better Living Magazine")

Two pictures designed and hooked by the author. Above: Dashing Lady. Below: Winter Moonlight.

Stair carpet with delightful Early American motifs including the eagle, Stars and Stripes, clipper ship, and the old homestead. The mixed color "paving" design on the stair treads is a practical device for minimizing the appearance of dirt and wear.

(Courtesy "Better Homes & Gardens")

Above: Nosegay rug, room size. A typical Victorian pattern with a trellis scroll, reproduced from an old design by the author. Below: Rose and Lily, 42 by 64 inches, designed and hooked by Beth Lucas.

(Photo: Vern Hamilton)

These are probably the most popular of all with those who hook rugs regularly, and they provide a wonderful opportunity to incorporate your favorite flowers. There is a fragile daintiness and graciousness in this type of rug that is indescribably lovely.

Placing the Centerpiece. To start a design, such as shown in fig. 79, first decide on the size of the rug, then allot a proportionate space for the flower centerpiece. A safe rule to use while establishing the size of the center design is to add 2 inches to half the length of the rug, and the same proportion for the width. Thus, in a 3 by 5-foot rug, the center grouping would be 32 inches long by 20 inches wide at the broadest parts of the design. This rule works well either for the oblong- or oval-shaped rug.

After establishing the widest parts of the center design on vellum paper according to the suggestions given above, connect these points, drawing an oval shape in the center of the pattern. Next, supposing you wish to have a varied floral grouping with roses predominating, you would plan either one or more roses in the center of the design. In the latter case, you would turn the roses so each was set at a graceful angle facing slightly outward from the center as shown in fig. 79. Other flowers and leaves are added next, working out from the center in a well-balanced arrangement. When your pencil sketch has been completed to your satisfaction, it is next transferred to the burlap, ready for hooking.

By drawing off individual samples of all the flowers to be represented in your rug, as suggested in the preceding chapter, it is an easy matter to slip these underneath the transparent vellum paper as you work to help you to arrive at the best placing. Add leaves where needed to fill in odd spaces, but be sure to leave some space occasionally for the background here and there, so your work won't look crowded.

The Scroll. The proper spacing for the scroll is about halfway between the widest or longest part of the central grouping of flowers, and the edge of the border—or, if anything, a little nearer to the border as in fig. 78. A curlicue scroll, like those found in many wallpapers is suitable for the framework of a floral grouping. Scrolls can also consist of conventionalized leaves arranged at alternating angles around the rug, or they may be composed of a wreath of scattered flowers, repeated from the central pattern.

CHANGING A COMMERCIAL PATTERN

Many times we like some parts of a commercial pattern but not others. In such cases we can change the unsatisfactory details to satisfy our individual taste. One hooker expressed her individuality by reshaping a rectangular rug into an oval one, encircling the commercial centerpiece with a wreath of hand-drawn flowers which she traced from the center. She did a wonderful job and the finished rug was a beauty. At other times

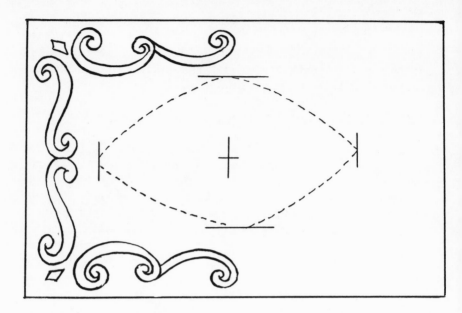

Fig. 78. An eighteenth-century pattern is started by marking center area and placing scroll.

Fig. 79. Completed eighteenth-century pattern showing suitable proportion.

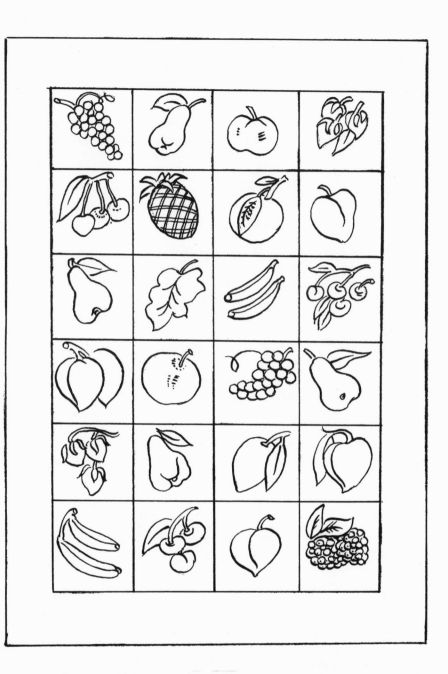

Fig. 80. Block pattern with fruit. Any fruit can be used and background for each square should be the same neutral color such as beige, gray, tan, or possibly green. Plaids, checks, or solid colors could be used. The lines dividing blocks should be in a strong dark color and you may need to hook these in double rows.

it may be that we wish to change certain flowers, or the general color scheme to suit the room in which the rug is to be placed.

VICTORIAN DESIGNS

These with their profusion of flowers and elaborate scrolls are more ornate in character than those of the eighteenth century. See page 131. Roses usually predominate, and pansies, forget-me-nots, calla lilies together with other rather splashy-colored flowers are hooked in brighter colors than those used in classic eighteenth-century designs, the latter usually being distinguished by the muted, dainty colorings featured in the famous French Aubusson carpets.

FRUIT DESIGNS

These were very popular during the Victorian era, too, both as a design for the center of a rug or as a wreathlike scroll. Large block patterns also sometimes featured fruit motifs, and this class of rug is also of Victorian origin. The design is particularly attractive when a different fruit is planned for each block as in fig. 80. Any number of variations can be worked out to suit your own requirements.

A very effective design is a wreath of fruit following the contour of an oval rug with a plain center. See fig. 81. Alternatively a grouping of autumn leaves might be placed in the center for a more full Victorian effect. Generally speaking, however, it is best to simplify Victorian designs to conform with contemporary tastes. Too much detail and color can result in a cluttered look not in keeping with current styles of decoration.

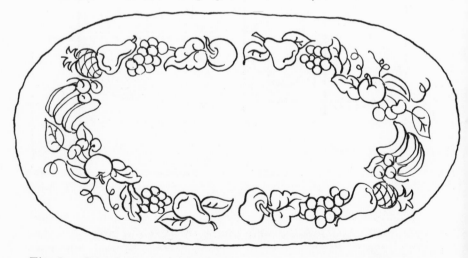

Fig. 81. Oval fruit pattern. Clusters of fruit are effective designed as a garland for an oval or circular rug.

24

DESIGNING PATTERNS FOR CHAIR SEATS AND FOOTSTOOLS

Hooking with yarn or strips of woolen material need not be confined to the making of rugs. Some of the prettiest and most practical covers for chairs, benches, or footstools are those fashioned in this manner. With a smaller area to hook, much less time and effort is required, and it is really a most enjoyable undertaking.

The hooking procedure is the same as for rug making, except that it is recommended that the loops should be made slightly lower for finer work. From ⅜ to ¼ inch is about right. Fine flannels cut into strips ⅛ inch wide are best for hooking the design, and many prefer to use all-wool jersey, cut lengthwise and about 3⁄16 inch wide, for the background. Covers can also be hooked in yarn using the hollow-handle hook as described in chapter 4.

When designing your own patterns, use vellum paper as for the rugs, assembling grouping of flowers or fruit from separate drawings or tracings, then transferring the completed design onto burlap as described in chapter 22. Burlap or monk's cloth is used for the foundation.

Ideas for suitable subjects can be discovered from many sources. For instance, for a dining-room chair seat cover, you might borrow the motif of a hand-painted plate. The study of needlepoint groupings or pictures are also sure to prove helpful.

A couple of large flowers with leaves, together with smaller flowers or buds makes a pretty floral grouping for a chair or footstool. Two roses as in fig. 82, or a rose and a poppy, with three large leaves, and two scattered

Fig. 82. Pattern for a chair seat cover or hooked picture.

groupings of violets or forget-me-nots with tiny leaves, makes a pleasing grouping. A larger design could also incorporate a calla lily, an iris, or a tulip.

For a round footstool, you might design a small wreath of flowers, such as three red roses along with tiny flowers of yellow and blue scattered in-between. A square or oblong seat or stool could be planned with the same flowers or fruit arranged in the square or oblong.

Many people search at auctions or antique shops for the old-fashioned sewing rockers or folding rockers as these are particularly well adapted to hooked or embroidered coverings. Not only the seats, but the backs of these chairs often permit the use of a hooked design. When planning both a seat and a back, these need not necessarily match in design, in fact they are often more interesting if they differ, provided there is some relationship between the two designs.

FRUIT PATTERNS FOR DINING-ROOM CHAIRS

Sets of patterns are often desired for dining-room chairs. While they may match exactly, it is much more interesting and more fun to hook when each one is slightly different. Fruit groupings are particularly suitable here and can be designed in each case to go on the same colored background so the entire set of chairs will be properly related. Fruit designs are scaled according to the size of the grouping. In other words, if several fruits are included in your pattern the design will have to be smaller in scale than if only one or two are featured. The following fruit combinations are suggested:

1. Pear, peach, grapes, strawberries, and autumn leaf.
2. Apple, plum, banana, strawberries, grapes, and autumn leaves. (See fig. 84.)

Fig. 83. This chair seat pattern, worked out in fruit, is particularly suitable for a set of dining-room chairs.

Fig. 84. Fruit design variation for a chair seat. This matches the design in fig. 83 and shows how a set of different but related designs can be worked out for the dining room.

3. Plum, pear, cherries, grapes, and autumn leaf.
4. Pears, strawberries, grapes, cherries, and autumn leaf. (See fig. 83.)
5. Green apple, banana, cherries, strawberries, and autumn leaf.
6. Peach, berries, green grapes, apple, and autumn leaf.

A good proportion for the size of such designs in relation to the background is shown in figs. 83 and 84.

A different set of chairs might be designed with a circular wreath of fruit, combining an apple, pear, peach, plum, and possibly small fruit such as cherries or berries, if space permits. Appropriate leaves should be inserted at intervals between the fruits.

A modern color scheme could be worked out with lemons and limes in a garland of dark green ivy leaves on a light gray background.

In working out fruit patterns it is necessary, as in the case of flowers, to plan the arrangement so that the colors will contrast pleasingly. Neutral green leaves are useful in between the various colors and you might then plan to have yellows next to reds or browns, rather than placing two shades of any color next to each other, such as a red apple against red strawberries, for instance.

A pink-cheeked peach with its yellow tones is lovely near dark red cherries or purple grapes, and a red apple is attractive near green grapes or a yellow banana. The violet tones of blackberries or plums contrast prettily with golden pears or green grapes and foliage.

FRUIT PATTERNS WITH BLOSSOMS

In antique fruit plates, we often see illustrations showing two similar fruits in different shadings. These are frequently accompanied by one or two branches with leaves, and sometimes blossoms as well. One set of fruit plates in a rare collection employs the following variations:

1. Three peaches grouped in a triangular manner, with blossoms on each side of the top peach.
2. A reddish pear and a yellow pear hanging from the same blossom-covered branch, with an arrangement of wine-red cherries at the base of the design.
3. A dark red apple, also one shading from yellow highlights into reds, side by side, with branches of blossoms slanting between the apples at the top, also at the base.
4. Three full purple plums, with two or three partly hidden behind them, along with two leaves and blossoms on one side and one blossom on the other.

These plate subjects are designed as companion pieces and, like many other antique sets, give us an excellent group of working designs to reproduce in chair seat patterns for a dining room. It is well worth exploring this field for source material, particularly as many designs can be traced on vellum paper directly from the plates.

FINISHING CHAIR SEATS OR OTHER COVERS

Hooked covers need no binding sewed on the edges. Cut the burlap about 1 inch from the hooked edge, turn once and hem by machine to prevent edges from fraying. Steam-press the finished piece just as for the hooked rug, and let it dry before fastening on chair.

ATTACHING PATTERN

Turn edges under as needed to fit the chair or stool, and use ordinary carpet tacks, hammering them in lightly while positioning the pattern on the chair. After it is correctly placed and shaped as desired, remove carpet tacks, one at a time, replacing each as removed with a regular upholstery tack, preferably of the brass-headed variety, with a round or hammered head.

Fruit picture hooked from
woolen strips by Sadie Lund.

25
YOU CAN HOOK A PICTURE, TOO

Hooking pictures for framing is both fascinating and easy, furthermore it takes comparatively little time. When made with narrow strips of woolen, hooked pictures can be every bit as effective as a folk painting. They may be as gay and alive with vivid coloring as you like, or soft and mellowed like an old print. Always they have a distinctive homespun appearance that is most appealing.

Nearly any subject that can be painted, needlepointed, embroidered, or cross-stitched may also be hooked. The most successful way for a beginner to start out is to copy a particular subject that takes his or her fancy. In this manner, all shading and coloring is already established, and may be copied in detail as work progresses. This is particularly recommended for scenes, such as old Currier and Ives prints, which lend themselves beautifully to this type of work. Color reproductions of primitive paintings, prints, or old embroidery in magazines or books, also Christmas cards, will almost surely provide the necessary inspiration.

Probably the easiest of all types of pictures for you to make will be the floral composition, that is if by now you have experienced hooking different kinds of flowers in rugs—or have had some previous experience in embroidery.

If making your own design, study a small needlepoint tapestry, or take your inspiration directly from a real bouquet of flowers. A common temptation here, however, is to overcrowd a picture. You will find it better to hook separate flowers, most of the time, rather than to attempt a massed arrangement with many flowers half hidden by others. This is the reason why in hooked pictures or needlework the arrangement and the shape of the flowers is often highly stylized—to make an interesting composition out of separate flowers and leaves. There are limitations in every art technique, but the charm lies in making a virtue out of necessity. Study folk embroideries for interesting ideas for this type of work.

Like fruit chair seat designs, hooked pictures of fruit are especially appropriate for the dining room. Smaller groupings than those suggested for the seat covers are usually desirable, as it may be best to keep hooked pictures on the small side especially at the beginning. Perhaps you may find an old print, or a quaint early American water color, depicting a colorful bowl or basket of fruit, which would lend itself to an attractive interpretation.

Other subjects you might select are birds or animals—an Audubon print, for instance, might form the basis for a colorful hooked picture, or one or another type of sporting print. If you are a budding Picasso or Braque you may prefer an abstract composition, relying on color and a balance of lines, squares, triangles, and circles. The technique is equally well adapted to this type of subject. Small scale hit-or-miss designs as in a patchwork quilt can also make an effective small picture—relying entirely on pattern, color, and texture for its effect in a modern setting.

The method of enlarging a picture for hooking was described in chapter 23, also shown by fig. 76. The same method, in reverse, can also be used for reducing the size. Tracings or original compositions on vellum paper are transferred to the canvas as described in the same chapter.

ATTACHING PATTERN TO FRAME

As in hooking rugs, a picture pattern must be stretched on a frame and securely fastened with tacks. Any kind of a frame can be used. If your regular rug frame is too large, an old picture frame will do, or a small frame can be quickly nailed together as described in chapter 2. If you have a frame that is smaller than the pattern, unhooked areas of the latter may always be moved over the frame as work progresses.

MATERIALS TO USE FOR A HOOKED PICTURE

Use various woolens—from your scrap bag, of course. Most all of the materials left over from rug hooking are likely to be needed, so you may as well have them handy. Better to have a lot of different scraps of color rather than a large quantity of one kind, so you have plenty of choice for a colorful picture. Of course, flannels are ideal—as always—for fine hooking, but other material such as tweed mixtures and sometimes all wool jerseys, serges, etc., can be used, too, for different shaded effects. It is true that nearly any material can be hooked into a picture—silks, rayons, cottons—but, from the author's point of view, by far the most pleasing results are obtained with woolens. There is no reason why you should not do some experimenting, however, as you may come up with a unique formula of your own. Much depends on how realistic and uniform in texture you wish your picture to be. To obtain certain special colors you may have to dye material and this can be done as described in chapter 13.

CUTTING STRIPS FOR PICTURE MAKING

Strips should be cut just as fine as possible without pulling apart when they are hooked. Fine cutting permits more detailed shading where required; it also results in a more pleasing texture within the small area of a picture. If using wool jersey, cut your strips wider than the other woolens since the material is likely to stretch when hooked. It is best to cut strips only as needed, except when working on larger areas where a considerable quantity of the same material is indicated.

WHAT HOOK TO USE

If you are used to doing fine work, then your regular hook should do. The author uses the same hook both for pictures and rugs. However, if there is any doubt in your mind, better not struggle with too large a hook, but get the finest one you can work with. This will result in neater work, which is particularly necessary in hooked pictures. However, don't try and obtain as small a hook, for instance, as a crochet hook for No. 80 thread, as then you will really be in trouble. A medium-fine hook should do the trick.

A FEW OTHER HINTS

When copying a print or painting, you will naturally be guided by the colors of the original, making certain necessary adaptations as you go along. When composing your own designs, certain of the shading ideas given earlier in the book may prove useful, and if you have already done some rug hooking you will have discovered many other devices of your own for color effects.

Your hooked picture may be a composite of several designs, so before deciding on each detail, study other pictures for interesting interpretations of skies, trees, or other subjects you plan to feature.

Always hook details before filling in expanses of background, such as a tree before a sky, an animal before a field, so that these outlines are properly established. If your composition includes a house, do the windows, shutters and doors before filling in the expanse of walls.

Don't be afraid to include people in your design if you feel so inclined. Sometimes they are easier to hook than they are to draw. To add life to your

Two pictures hooked by the author. Above: Home on the Mississippi adapted from a Currier and Ives print. Below: The Sleigh Ride, recently reproduced commercially in color on a Christmas card.

picture it is best to have them doing something, rather than standing about. Always outline them first, before doing a surrounding background, so the correct contours will be retained. By studying originals you will soon become adept at copying highlights and shadows. A word of advice—you will find faces in profile much easier to hook than those looking straight out of the picture. In small details like this, you may sometimes find it necessary to push the loops slightly one way or another. Be careful not to let backgrounds crowd details out of shape.

Subtle coloring always wears better than very bright or harsh colors. The purpose of your hooked picture is not to look like a poster. Bright colors are fine in small quantities, however, and may give just the right touch of liveliness—a red shirt on a figure, perhaps, or a bright blue scarf or skirt, but even then such colors should be in harmony with the rest of the picture. Backgrounds other than scenic interpretations are best in neutral shades, just as they are in rugs. Beiges, tans, grays, or antique white are great standbys.

Color series will often come in handy not only in flower pictures but also for such details as people's clothing, when realism is desired. For instance, the darker color would be used for outlining, followed by two or three shades of lighter material for the highlights of a contour. All one shade produces a flat effect which is quite permissible if that is the type of folk picture you want.

You may need any amount of color before you are through hooking a picture, so keep all your scraps handy. One of the author's pictures used more than 150 colors and shades.

While you will discover your own preferences as you select colors, the following are a few suggestions for certain details.

Evergreen trees are realistic when shaded in cool greens with a blue cast, while the summer foliage of maples and other trees may require both the blue greens for shadows and yellow greens for highlights. Autumn foliage is best hooked with spot-dyed material as described in chapter 15.

In winter scenes, most buildings should be hooked in muted pastel shades. In rural settings, however, the farmyard almost steals the show when the weathered barn is done in muted red rose. Fences are best in black or brown to contrast with the snow, which is worked in off-white with gray to blue shadowing. Barren winter trees are shaded all the way from dark to light brown, with branches in the lightest shade toward the ends. Skies may be filled in with light gray with a bluish cast.

Summer scenes, of course, feature greens instead of snow-covered areas. Fences are best hooked in white, for better contrast; buildings are hooked in muted pastels or off-white, with the exception of the classic red barn; skies can be bluer if desired. In either a winter or summer scene, clouds should be hooked before doing the sky. If they are not drawn beforehand, use crayons to trace billowy outlines freehand on the burlap. Use shades of darker gray than that used in the sky for shadowed clouds, off-white for the main area and touches of pure white, perhaps, for certain highlights. The bluer your sky, the lesser the amount of gray used and the lighter the shade. Never hook clouds in straight lines, but use curving lines as you fill in for a more natural effect. The sky can also be hooked in curves, or straight if you prefer.

Sunsets are as precarious a subject for the hooker as they are for the painter, but if you want to take the plunge, use a small amount of burnt orange at the horizon line, followed by bright yellow into fainter yellows as it blends into gray or blue toward the top of the picture. Add dashes of yellow in among the blues or grays of the upper part of the sky to keep it from being too heavy. A pink glow in the sunset can be obtained by using soft pink materials with a peach cast, instead of the orange, and working this into the gray-blue sky as above, without the strips of yellow.

If there are trees or mountains in the far distance of a sunset picture, it is effective to shade them in mauve tones near the horizon. In the foreground, grass or foliage should be in dark gray-greens, and buildings or other details in soft muted tones that suggest the time of day.

Rocks and streams occur in many landscapes. For shading rocks, grays dyed in series with a lavender cast are most attractive. For water, use cool blue-greens shading from light to dark and you might add touches of light yellow or gold here and there to add movement.

Don't be bashful about signing and dating your picture. Leave room for this in the lower right- or left-hand corner of the work, whichever side has less detail. If there is not room for your name, add your initials at least. Outline the signature or initials with crayon directly on the burlap before you fill in the background. For outlining the writing, loops should be very fine and of a contrasting color to the surrounding background. Black is usually the best color to select, but sometimes dark brown ties in better with the general color scheme. If the coloring of the picture is very dark toward the bottom, then a lighter color, matching some other detail in the composition, will be a wiser choice. If your subject has some particular family or historic interest, paste a short typewritten legend to the back of the frame.

PREPARING PICTURE FOR FRAMING

Trim off excess burlap within 1 or 1½ inches of the hooked work, double-fold the edges under and hem by machine. You should then have a very small hem left on each side for attaching it to the back of a permanent wall frame. Before framing, steam-press the hooked work with reverse side up just as you do for a hooked rug.

There is no need for glass over the picture, as the hooked texture looks best uncovered. Attach the hemmed edges of the burlap to the frame by means of numerous thumbtacks or small carpet tacks, stretching the picture tightly from all directions, so it does not bag at any point. Attach screw eyes to the back of the frame, one on each side a little above center, and fasten picture wire through them so your picture is ready to hang on the wall. Another successful way to hang the picture is to place one screw eye slightly below the top center on the backside of the frame. Bend screw eye after it is screwed into the wood so that the ring top extends outward at a slight angle for convenient hanging on the nail. In this way the picture is hung with only one screw eye and no wire at all. If the screw eye is screwed into the wood at about ½ inch from the top it will not show at all when the picture is hung, and the picture lies perfectly flat on the wall. Place the screw eye in the exact center or the picture will hang crooked.

CHOOSING THE RIGHT FRAME

Deeper moldings do more for hooked subjects than the flat type of frame. Walnut, chestnut, or other natural wood frames are good for general use, and a band of gold on the inner edge sets the work off to great advantage. You can leave the rest of the wood in its natural state and just wax it, or for a darker finish, stain the wood, then varnish or shellac. All-gold frames can be used for traditional designs, while more stylized or modern subjects look best in frames painted gray, white, or another light color that is appropriate to the general overall shading of the picture. If you want to make your own frame or do your own finishing, there is an excellent work on the market entitled *Better Frames for Your Pictures* by Frederic Taubes.

Don't frame your hooked picture in a frame with thin molding as the result will look top heavy. A good width of molding for pictures up to 15 by 25 inches is around 2 to 3 inches. The larger pictures need the 3-inch width for a shadow-box effect.

If you are in the habit of going to local auction sales, here is a good tip. Watch out for old framed pictures. When the subject of the picture is unattractive, stained, or outdated, these usually go for a song and many attractive frames can be procured in this way for the fraction of the cost of a new one. Remove the old print from the picture and use this as a guide for the size of burlap, allowing enough coverage for tacking to the frame. Thus you can plan your next picture to fit the frame you have. Don't be put off if certain old frames look a bit grubby, for it is easy to clean or refinish them, provided they are otherwise in good shape and are basically attractive.

Perhaps the most sought after frame today for the hooked picture is the solid walnut Victorian frame of the shadow-box type. The molding of this frame runs from 2 to 3½ inches wide and the frame is almost as deep. It usually has a gold liner which sets off the work to perfection.

26

HOW TO BRAID A RUG FROM START TO FINISH

Like rug hooking, the art of braiding is one of our oldest handicrafts, handed down by our grandmothers and great-grandmothers who knew how to make the most of their possessions. The braided rugs they created from discarded woolens were not only inexpensive to make but they were beautiful and practical too, lasting for years and years. For the same reason, today, a well-made hand-braided rug is worth far more than any machine-made equivalent with its mechanical evenness and poorer lasting qualities. Besides being easy to make, yet another advantage of the hand-braided rug is that just about any kind of woolen may be used in it. So here is a chance to use up materials you found it advisable to eliminate from your other rugs.

Braided rugs combine beautifully in a room with hooked rugs, further-more certain early or primitive designs can be hooked, and a braided border added around the edge. More about this will be found later on.

MATERIALS FOR BRAIDING

As in your hooked rugs, it's best to use only all-wool materials, but as already suggested, your choice is wider here, particularly if long and heavy wear is not anticipated. In this case even cotton can be used. Among the woolen materials tweed suits and the heavier serges, are just as appropriate for our purpose as the other woolens particularly recommended for hooking. Your choice therefore, among old overcoats, suits, sport coats, bathrobes, slacks, skirts, stoles, scarves, blankets, and other garments or coverings is wide indeed, though you should discriminate against very flat and thin serges or gabardines, the wearing qualities of which are likely to be below par.

Heavy woolens, such as coats with a furry texture, have the best wearing qualities, and are ideal for braiding, but a combination of various woolen materials make a very satisfactory braided rug in the true tradition.

Rugs braided from old materials last a lifetime when they are well made, aided by the fact that with little variation on the two sides, they can be reversed periodically for longer wear in a room. The author's braided rugs have all been made from various old woolens in informal though preplanned color schemes. Some braiders prefer to buy all new materials, and there is nothing against this, of course, except the cost. Although such rugs may prove to last a little better through the years, this is questionable when older materials in good condition are selected. The chief advantage in using new materials really lies in the fact that it is easier to select materials the exact color you want, whereas if you rely on whatever is handy, your choice may be confined to a hit-or-miss pattern. Even in the latter case, certain colors can be chosen to carry out a preplanned color scheme, and there is always the possibility of dyeing materials or buying certain new pieces to complete the color range desired.

The braided rug traditionally lends itself so well to an informal atmosphere that it is really best not to plan too set a coloring. In others words, not only is it permissible occasionally to introduce a harmonious mixture or color other than that formally prescribed, but this is actually desirable for that well-loved "homey" look, which makes homemade rugs more subtle and less hard looking than machine-made ones. Spontaneous, quaint, irregular touches of color give a rug individual character.

As for hooking, old materials selected for braiding must first be washed out thoroughly and have all seams ripped apart.

To achieve a balanced color scheme, use both bright and subdued colors. The arrangement of color should be planned in advance as far as possible, with most, if not all, of the material on hand when braiding commences. Although a rug may always be enlarged later on as additional material is collected, at least the predominating colors must be established and enough material in these shades collected at the outset. Materials can be dyed as described in chapter 14 if necessary, making sure sufficient noniodized salt is used in the dye solution for setting the color permanently.

In dyeing braided materials it is advisable to cable the woolen before dyeing it. After material is cabled, loop it into a circle measuring about 15 inches, and tie a twine string around it so as to hold it in order while

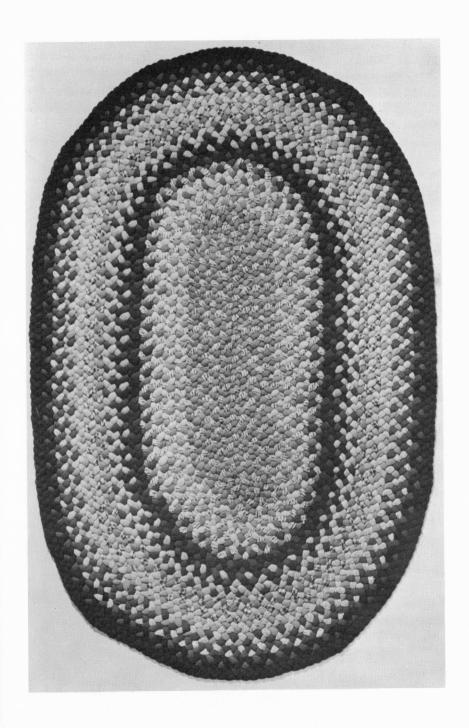

Braided Throw Rug, 3 by 5 feet, made by Opal Cramer. The colors featured are beiges, greens, and browns.

it is being dyed. It is handy to hang for drying when tied in such a way. After it is dyed and is dry, roll the cabling into a ball as usual.

When planning a color scheme, it is best to follow the rule of placing lighter shades in the center, for the start of the rug, and then work into the darker colors by degrees, thereafter alternating between the light and dark. As a beginning, for instance, you might select the following—a beige or tan, a brown check or tweed mixture, and a pastel yellow. This makes a beautiful center, though another group of three light colors could just as easily be selected for a different color scheme.

The size of the center in light colors may vary according to the size planned for the finished rug—also according to individual taste. A small rug may have only five, seven, or nine rows of similar braiding in the center, whereas a large room-size rug may have twenty-five or thirty rows. This doesn't mean that we can't change from one material to another within a large center if we need or want to. For instance, a beige may be changed into a slightly darker material if we run out of the first color, or the brown check may be substituted with a larger check or even a brown tweed as we work outward. It is best to stop such changes at the end of a complete round for the sake of uniformity. Therefore, if material starts to run out, don't begin another round that can only be a quarter or half finished. We will go more fully into the question of colors later on.

To estimate whether a strip will braid around the rug, measure cabling, allowing twice around the rug. That is, if the strip will stretch around the edge twice before braiding it should be sufficient to braid around the edge. If your strip is much less do not use it, unless you have another very similar material that may be joined on. Often material of slightly different coloring may be joined on and will show no difference at all after being braided and laced. In this way every bit of cabling may be used to best advantage.

DO WE HAVE TO MAKE CABLES FOR BRAIDING?

Many say no, but the author recommends it as the best procedure, for thicker rugs, at least. A cable is really a strip of material prepared for braiding by folding (lengthwise) each side toward the center, then folding in half again and sewing together at the edges with long blind stitches. Though it takes time to sew cables, the actual braiding process is more efficiently and quickly done without having to contend with the raw edges of folded unsewed strips.

For people eager to braid a rug as quickly as possible, a braiding kit is now offered on the market. This kit consists of an aluminum or steel lacing needle and a set of three metal clamps, each of which is a disk-like cylinder device with edges bent over in such a manner as to fold torn strips automatically while drawn through. See fig. 85. The three steel devices are kept near the point of braiding, and are easily pulled along as you braid. However, in order to use it properly, woolen strips must be uniform, as

(Photo: Max Tatch)

Braided dining room rug, 8 by 10 feet, made by Elsie Hutchinson. Colors begin with ten rows in red, navy, brown tweed, with dark bands, alternating as it enlarges, in navy blue. Other colors introduced are gray, black, green, gold, and many tans and mixtures.

Fig. 85. Device for folding cables while braiding.

only one width is possible. While beautiful braided rugs can be made by using these folding clamps, the main objection is that the size of the openings only allows for a narrow braid, and consequently a thin rug results. Until they are manufactured to carry wider strips, they cannot be whole-heartedly accepted. The big advantage of the automatic folder, of course, is the time it saves in making cables, and this may outweigh the main objections for some people. Furthermore, one clamp can sometimes be used for extra-heavy material in combination with two other hand-folded or basted strips. This is possible because the narrower width of extra heavy material might frequently equal each of the two wider strips that require hand folding and basting into cables before braiding.

BRAIDING A RUG WITH AN AUTOMATIC FOLDER

There are numerous types of automatic folders for quick braiding. The one shown in fig. 85 is a typical example and operates as follows:
1. Strips of 1¾-inch width are torn or cut and the ends are tapered by cutting so that they will thread through the folders. Pull different-colored material through each of the three folders about 3 inches, then sew the three ends together. Fasten the sewed ends to some object so strips can be held easily and will hang down without tangling. Now begin braiding as for braiding hair, pulling down the automatic folders far enough so braiding can proceed conveniently.
2. When braid nears the end of the strips, sew on additional strips, always cutting and sewing them on the bias. A firm grasp on the folder will pull the sewed seams through.
3. For thinner material it is sometimes possible to place a small extra strip within the regular strip for equalizing its weight. Check this added strip occasionally to make sure it is kept in place for a neat fold.

When using these automatic folders for braiding, a very heavy weight material, such as ladies' or men's overcoats, is advisable. This will result in a medium-weight braided rug.

OTHER METHODS OF BRAIDING

Many very successful at braiding advocate just hand-folding strips as they are braided without sewing them into cables. Others believe the best way is to pin the strips in the correct fold a short way ahead as they braid, the suggested distance being about twelve or fifteen inches. In both these ways, as when using the automatic folder, the task of preparing cables is avoided. It is suggested that the reader try each method to discover his or her own preference. For those wishing to follow the author's method, which is the traditional one, notes on making cables follow.

MAKING CABLES FOR BRAIDING

Whether to tear or cut material depends on the weave of the material. Some will tear beautifully, while others of loose weave require cutting. You will soon discover which procedure must be followed with each piece. The width of strips may vary from 1¾ inches to 3 or more inches in width, depending on the thickness of the material. Extra-heavy material should be torn about 1¾ inches wide; heavy material 2 inches; medium weight about 2½ inches; lightweight about 3 to 4 inches, depending upon thickness. For example, an extra-heavy coat makes 1¾-inch strips; a medium-

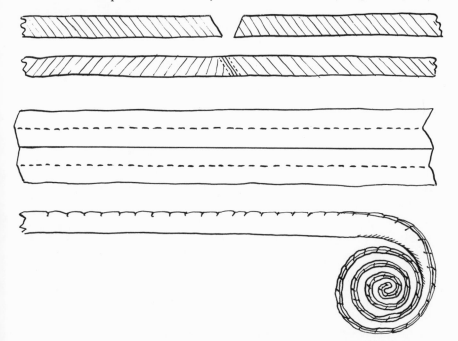

Fig. 86. Top: Strips cut on bias and sewed together for cables. Center: How strips are folded to make cable. Bottom: As edges of strips are sewed together to form cable, roll cable into balls for easy braiding.

weight coat makes strips of 2 or 2½ inches, depending upon exact weight; while a medium- or light-weight bathrobe may require strips of perhaps 3 inches in width. Sometimes, in order not to waste material, you may bolster lightweight material by placing a smaller matching strip inside the cable as you fold. The main point to remember is to achieve equalized cables, no matter what width or weight of material is used. The idea is to tear strips in such widths that, when they are made into cables by folding each side toward the center, then folding once again, and basted, they come out in equal widths of about ¾ inches. For even braiding each of your three lengths must be of the same proportions, just as you would separate hair evenly into three strands before commencing to braid it.

You will find a 6-inch ruler invaluable when measuring strips for tearing. Mark off widths along the entire top edge of a large piece of material, notching or clipping each point where a tear is to be made. You will save much time and effort this way, tearing strips in one successive operation.

SEWING STRIPS TOGETHER

After tearing or cutting strips in correct width, sew ends together on the bias, as shown in fig. 86, preferably by machine. The most orderly method is to finish doing one color and kind of material at a time, particularly if using old woolens. You can then clearly see the limits of your collection in each type of material and coloring. If there is a difference in the right and wrong side of material, be sure to have the best side facing out. Always sew the strips together with matching thread and with the raw seams on the underside. Make cables as long as you wish.

BASTING THE CABLE

Strips are basted as you fold them lengthwise into cables. Again use a matching or neutral thread, also a milliner's needle to make long blind stitches about an inch long. While basting each color, roll the cables into balls, so they are neat and easy to use when braiding begins. Keep the rolled cables in separate boxes according to color and type of material so your selection is facilitated as color changes are made during braiding. Make a number of balls in each desired color, not forgetting beige, tan, or other neutral colors for blending with brighter ones. Plaids and checks also blend well with solid colors and add an interesting texture.

THE BRAIDING PROCESS

Choose your three light colors to start the center, trying out different combinations until you find the one you like best. Sew the ends of two cables together on the reverse side, so no seams show. Lap the end of the third cable over the right side of the seam of the other two cables, tucking the raw edge inside, then baste securely with blind stitches. The three cables should form a T shape as shown in fig. 87. You are now ready to begin braiding. Fold the left cable toward you over the center cable, then fold the right cable over the one just folded. Pull each fold tight to make a hard, firm braid. Continue folding cables in this manner, just as you would braid hair, pulling each cable just as tight as possible with seams always at cables' edge, as folds are made. Don't let seams work to the middle of the cables.

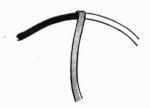

Fig. 87. Three cables are sewed together to form T before braiding begins.

If the braid is clamped to a table directly after it is begun, you will find it handier to work especially at the beginning. You may also find it easier to keep the cables straight if you stand while braiding.

Let two of the balls of cable lie on the floor, unwinding as you braid. The third ball (choose the smallest, if there is variation in lengths) can be pinned up with a safety pin about 18 or 20 inches from the point where you are braiding. The last ball may then be worked easily around the remaining two cables, operating back and forth like a shuttle while the other two cable lengths lie on the floor. After braiding has proceeded for a while, it may be necessary to change to another ball, pinning it up as you did the first, to keep free from twisted the cables on the floor. All three balls, pinned up in turn, can thus be kept straight and orderly as you braid. When you stop braiding, use a clamp clothespin to hold the end of the braid, thus preventing your work from loosening.

LACING THE BRAIDS

By this time you will have decided what size and shape to make the rug. The basic center is determined by the difference between the length and the width of the finished rug. For instance, if you wish a 6-by-8-foot rug, the basic center would be 2 feet long. Or a 9-by-12-foot rug has a basic center of 3 feet.

For the oval rug, which is usually the most popular choice, the basic center is figured by taking the length of the braid at turning point (see fig. 88). For the round braided rug, no basic center is required. Lacing for

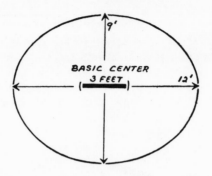

Fig. 88. Illustration showing proportion of basic center in a braided rug.

the latter is begun by allowing 3 outside loops to 1 inside loop. As the rug progresses, less allowance is needed.

For lacing, use a 4-inch sack needle with a curved point. This is obtainable at hardware stores. Before using, the sharp point should be filed down to a blunt end. The needle should never penetrate the material, lacing being done underneath the loops of cable. Use extra-heavy waxed thread. Linen thread is best, and baseball thread or upholsterer's twine is excellent. Lay coils of braid in place and start lacing together.

For an oval rug, have the braid long enough to bend sideways at the basic point when you begin lacing, and with the braiding end nearest you. This throws the basic center on the right side so that you don't have to reach across the rug to lace the loops as it grows larger. Also be sure to lace with the same side up as you braid, for it is twice as hard to lace braiding from the wrong side.

To begin the work of lacing, loop thread through the inside cable at the fold, which is at the end of the basic center (fig. 90), and tie the ends

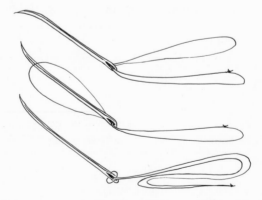

Fig. 89. Threading needle in the most convenient way for lacing the braided rug.

of the thread securely around the cable, pulling the knot underneath the loop of the braid. Always use double thread. To thread needle, slip the end of the loop of the double thread far enough through the eye of the needle so that you can insert the needle through the center of the loop, thus making a slip knot which may be released easily when more thread is

Fig. 90. How to begin lacing an oval braid.

to be added. See fig. 89. Stop using the thread when the remainder is a little longer than the needle. This will allow you to undo the slipknot at the eye. Join another loop of thread to the old loop by means of a slipknot and fasten this new loop to the needle in the same way. Now you are ready again to slipknot the thread on the needle as you did first. This method of threading makes knotting of only two threads necessary, where four threads are fastened together, and it works like a charm, retaining uniform length without tangling the thread. You may work with 3- or 4-yard lengths of double thread when you become accustomed to lacing.

To lace means to work back and forth from one braid to the other by going under each loop between the two edges, skipping none, and drawing the thread very tightly so that absolutely no thread is visible between the loops. Lacing is usually hard on the hands until you become used to it. A good idea is to stick adhesive tape on your fingers. After lacing for a while it will be obvious where such protection is needed. Gloves serve the same purpose, if preferred. After this protection at the beginning, you will soon find such precautions are no longer necessary.

When turning at the end of the basic center, lace two outside loops to one inside loop in order to add fullness for a smooth turn. Do this three times at the end to keep the braid flat: once just before reaching the end, then directly on the end, and the last double just after the end allowance. Thereafter, on the turn, you must estimate just enough extra loops to make a smooth turn without cupping or fullness.

Lay the rug flat on a table, and pin ahead with a safety pin to gauge the amount of extra outside loops needed to turn curve as the rug increases. Work to keep the rug so it lies perfectly flat at all times with no bulges or fullness. An old flatiron placed on the rug helps to hold it on the table as you are braiding, and makes lacing easier too. This method of lacing and braiding is done on the right side of the rug, although there should be little or no difference between the two sides. As the rug increases in size, you can roll up the opposite end to which you are lacing so table space is saved. In this way a very large rug can be braided on a table.

For greater convenience as you work at braiding, additional cabling, as needed, may be sewed on by hand, always on the bias, of course. Any splicing by hand must be sewed securely for strength in wear. Always change colors of the braids on the curve near the end, in approximately the same location each time, as such changes are less obvious. For a more even blending never change more than two cables at one time.

If there is any cupping in the rug, this should be corrected by unlacing some of the braiding and carefully relacing to adjust the tension. Sometimes cupping can be corrected by stretching a wet Turkish towel over the bulge, and then placing a weight, such as a piece of marble or other heavy flat object over the towel, and leaving overnight or until dry. This usually sets the rug so it lies in the proper shape—the woolens shrinking into place. Never continue your rug until any such marked tension is corrected.

FINISHING THE BRAIDED RUG

In finishing a braided rug, use dark rows or at least two dark cables braided with one light cable for at least three rows, and possibly five or seven in a very large rug. This achieves a finished effect like that of a framed picture. When the rug is the desired size, stop the braid by pigtailing the end. This is done on the curve at about the same location as you changed colors. Trim the last 6 or 8 inches of each of the three cables of the braid to a point; then fold and rebaste. Braid this pigtail to the end in a slim point and fasten securely with thread. Lace the loops as usual. The end of the pigtail must be tucked underneath a cable loop and fastened securely with thread. Use the point of a pair of scissors to push the end tightly out of sight. It is also possible to fasten the pigtail securely by lacing around it and continuing backward a few inches after reaching the end. Your rug should taper off so that only on close inspection can the end be seen.

27

COLOR SCHEMES FOR BRAIDED RUGS (ROOM SIZE, HALL, RUNNER, AND THROW RUGS)

Perhaps the greatest problem for those contemplating the making of a braided rug is how to work out a pleasing color scheme and how and when to change colors. The following color scheme used for the 9-by-11-foot braided rug shown on page 191 may suggest a suitable color scheme or order of light and dark and neutral colors for yours.

The rug we are taking for our example was planned to go in a room with maple and early American furnishings. The featured colors were reds, browns, greens, and yellows. This meant that many tans, checks, tweeds, also light and neutral colors were needed for blending purposes. Otherwise the rug would have been overpoweringly bold.

It will be noted that even though certain colors dominated, every braid in this rug, except the last five rows of dark brown, included one of the following colors: beige, tan, light yellow, or light green. Their use achieved a pleasing and uniform overall coloring.

This rug, which took three months to finish, was made entirely of old materials. The row-by-row color scheme is as follows:

30 rows: beige, brown check, yellow (center)
 1 row: gold, blue-green, beige
 1 row: green, brown, gold
 2 rows: dark green, brown, beige
 4 rows: tan, terra cotta, medium green
 2 rows: medium green, red, beige
 2 rows: tan, red, green, blue plaid
 1 row: red, tan, blue

1 row: red, tan, brown
3 rows: tan, brown, dark green
1 row: dark green, yellow, orange plaid
2 rows: yellow, blue-green, orange plaid
2 rows: gold, brown check, light green
2 rows: rust, chartreuse, brown tweed
1 row: red, green, brown check
1 row: red, green, tan check
3 rows: tan, brown, green tweed
2 rows: yellow, green check, brown tweed
3 rows: yellow, tan, brown check
1 row: light green, chartreuse, terra cotta
1 row: light green, red, tan
2 rows: medium green, red, tan
1 row: red, green, brown
1 row: brown, red, brown
5 rows: all brown

Another braided rug recently finished by the author was designed to go in the same room as a hooked rug inspired by a Dresden plate. Taking a cue from these the color scheme for the braided rug resulted in the use of pinks and wines, along with beiges, light blues—also navy blue. Tweeds and plaids were incorporated to soften the solid colorings. Measuring 35 by 60 inches, and with a basic center of 25 inches, the rug was built up as follows:

4 rows: beige, pink, light green (center)
2 rows: beige, pink, brown
1 row: beige, brown, wine
1 row: brown, navy blue, wine
2 rows: navy, wine, pastel plaid
1 row: wine, plaid, light blue
2 rows: plaid, light blue, tweed mixture
2 rows: dark red, plaid, tweed mixture
2 rows: medium wine, dark wine, tweed mixture
1 row: wine, pink, tweed mixture

For a rather dark long hallway with a sage-green paper, a long narrow braided runner was planned in reds, yellows, Scotch plaids, and various greens. The runner measured 10 feet long by 30 inches wide and was braided in the following combinations:

4 rows: beige, medium green, Scotch plaid
2 rows: beige, dark green, Scotch plaid
2 rows: yellow, chartreuse, Scotch plaid
2 rows: Scotch plaid, red, gray mixture
1 row: red, dark gray, brown mixture

2 rows: brown mixture, light blue, Scotch plaid
1 row: gray, light blue, Scotch plaid
2 rows: red, gray, plaid
1 row: red, yellow, light green mixture
1 row: light green mixture, yellow, dark green
2 rows: green, brown mixture, dark green

From the foregoing examples, the reader should have a good idea how to set about planning the color scheme for a braided rug. It's a good idea to make a chart of your color scheme before commencing, maybe trying out one or two color combinations on small braided lengths before you start in earnest.

Remember that centers of multicolored rugs are best kept light, that neutral colors are useful for braiding in with two contrasting colors, that you should tie your rug color scheme in with the other room furnishings. After the light center is completed, introduce a change by alternating one color, or never more than two at one time, so there will be no sudden breaks. Colors must change gradually. It is usually most desirable to have more lighter rows than dark—about half as many rows including dark, perhaps. Study actual examples of braided rugs for further ideas.

Braided rug for a den, by the author, described on page 189.

28

COMBINATION HOOKED AND
BRAIDED RUGS

The combination braided and hooked rug makes a pleasant change from the all-hooked rug. In the old days this type was also desirable from the practical standpoint because the braided border could easily be replaced with a new one when it became worn. Although a braided border can be added to any rug, it is of course best when an entire combination rug is planned from the start. The primitive and Colonial patterns are always a good choice for the center as the simpler or more informal the floral subject, the better the finished rug will look when the braided frame is added. The quaint little stair tread scenes, such as those illustrated opposite, are quickly made and make an ideal combination of the two techniques.

Should you wish to design your own combination rug, plan the center on vellum paper first, just as for any other hooked piece, then transfer this onto the burlap. Be as original as you like, remembering that the attraction of this type of design is its informality. No perfection of drawing is called for.

As in planning the all-braided rug, the length and width of the finished rug will retain the same proportion as the center. For instance, if the hooked center is 2-by-3-feet, and a 6-inch braided border is added, the finished rug with braided border will be 3-by-4-feet. Braided borders may also be attached to round, oblong, or oval rugs, the finished outline following the same contour as the hooked center.

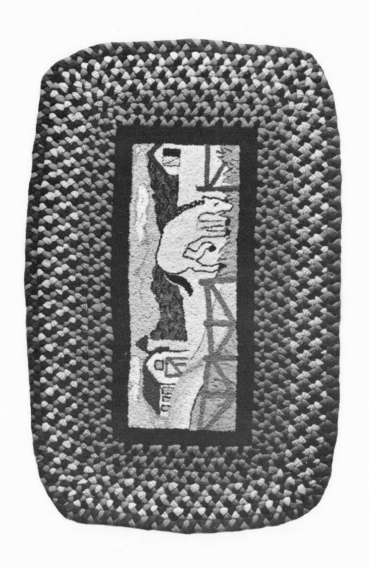

Combination hooked and braided rug, made by the author for a stair carpet. Colors featured are red, black, blue, and tan with touches of green in picture. Tweeds and checks are used in the braiding as well as solid colors.

HEM HOOKED-RUG CENTER BEFORE ADDING BRAIDING

Preferably before hooking the center, otherwise after hooking is finished, sew rug binding to the edge of the canvas. The rug at this stage must be hemmed and steam-pressed so as to lie perfectly flat before braiding is added.

PREPARING BRAIDING FOR THE BORDER

Follow the instructions in chapter 26 for assembling suitable braiding materials and prepare cables in the usual way. A few feet of braiding should be done before attaching to the hooked center—as described shortly.

At the beginning of the braided border, you may use cables that match, contrast, or blend with the edge of the hooked center—whichever you prefer. You might choose to braid two dark cables with one in tan to blend with a hooked center with a tan background, for instance. Also it is very effective to begin the braided part with all three cables alike and in a dark color. This creates the impression of a frame around a central design. Do this for perhaps three rows, then, in the fourth row, introduce one light cable, braiding it with two of the same dark ones. Follow this in the fifth row with two light and one dark cable, and in the sixth with all light ones. If more braiding is desired, you may alternate shades in reverse, again working back to the dark color with which you began.

Don't hesitate to use mixtures, such as plaids, tweeds, and checks, all of which are equally suitable in the combination rug. For an overall harmonious effect, it is a good rule to match colors used in the hooked part when planning your braiding materials.

ATTACHING THE BRAIDED BORDER

Start braiding as instructed in chapter 26. When the braid is about 2 or 3 feet long, begin lacing it to the hooked center. For the actual lacing together of the braids, use the coarse curved sack needle with the blunted point as recommended earlier. However, when sewing the braid to the hooked part, you will need to use a coarse darning needle. This will penetrate the hooked part, whereas the blunt sack needle won't. It will therefore take longer to attach the first row of braiding, as you have to change back and forth, first using the sack needle for the braiding, then changing to the ordinary needle for sewing the same thread through the hooked work. Be sure to thread the sack needle as recommended in chapter 26 so it is easily released as you alternate back and forth with the ordinary needle.

On an oblong rug, it is best to begin attaching the braid at one corner. If oval, begin about halfway between the central points of the end and side of the rug. On round rugs, it makes no difference where you begin. From here on, work as for an all-braided rug. Keep your work as flat and smooth as possible. If laced part draws too tightly or gathers, release needle and unlace thread as far back as necessary, then start over again.

The length of thread to use for lacing should be as long as possible. A beginner may use about 3 feet of double thread, but more experienced braiders should easily be able to lace with 5 or 6 feet.

In the oblong or square rug, colors are always changed on the same corner. In oval or round rugs, too, colors should be changed at the point where the braid begins, or thereabouts. When your braided border is wide enough, pigtail the end to a fine point, finishing a round at the spot where braiding began.

LINING

You will find that the braided part of your rug will be thicker than the hooked center. Therefore, it is necessary to line the hooked part with burlap. If it is much thinner, two or three thicknesses of burlap may be needed. Cut burlap to cover the center of the rug at the back, allowing a margin for turning under. With edges turned under and touching the first braid, sew on by hand. You will find it convenient to pin the burlap first so it lies perfectly flat. Sometimes the turned edge must be ironed flat so it will be easier to sew.

If there is any unevenness after attaching the lining, place a wet towel over the top surface of the rug and lay a flat, heavy and even weight over it for twelve hours or so. This pressing should apply only to the braided border, as the hooked part will already have been steam-pressed after completion.

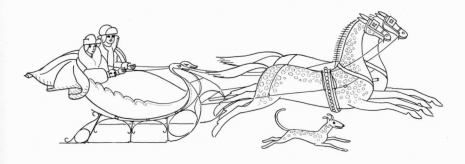

Line drawing based on a Currier and Ives motif, suitable for the center of a combination hooked and braided rug, or for a hooked picture (see chapter 25).

29

CARE OF YOUR HOOKED AND BRAIDED RUGS

PAD UNDER RUGS

Small hooked or braided rugs may be used on bare floors as well as on carpeting without padding, but hooked rugs of 3 by 5 feet or larger wear better if a waffle cushion is placed underneath them. Because of the excessive thickness of braided rugs they do not require the waffle cushion. However, without this protection from underneath the nap on hooked rugs will be flattened, shortening the life of the rug and never allowing it to look its best. Furthermore, an underpadding gives the vacuum cleaner a chance to do a much more thorough sweeping job.

VACUUMING HOOKED RUGS

With a vacuum cleaner there is no real cleaning problem, for all woolen rugs have great soil resistance. Vacuum your hooked or braided rugs just as often as you would any other rug and give the reverse side a going over, too, every once in a while. Rugs that stand much traffic should be vacuumed once a day.

CLEANING SPOTS

Occasional spots should be removed as soon as possible with a reliable spot cleaner. Never let your rug go until it becomes excessively soiled.

By cleaning an occasional spot as soon as possible, it will be easier and more successively removed. Old stains or spots are sometimes nearly impossible to eradicate.

PERIODIC DRY CLEANING

During the summer months it's a good idea to give thought to a major rug-cleaning operation. Just before fall seems the ideal time, since rugs usually get the most wear and tear through the summer months. Once a year should be the minimum cleaning and twice a year is recommended for a much-used rug.

Although your prize rugs may be sent out to be dry cleaned, if you feel like the author, you would rather do it yourself. There are many fine cleaners who do reputable work, but when you do your own cleaning, you are certain that the utmost care is being taken of your prized possessions.

Glamorene is a new rug cleaner which differs in many respects from other solvents. It is a dampish crumbly substance that is sprinkled on, then brushed with a stiff brush. When the surface is dry, the rug is vacuumed. This is a powerful and fast-acting cleaner but noninjurious and noninflammable. One gallon of Glamorene will clean four or five 9-by-12-foot rugs.

There are rug-cleaning solvents sold under brand names in the stores. These are good and very inexpensive. A couple of gallons of solvent will clean perhaps six or more rugs, depending on their size. All you need beside the solvent are clean Turkish towels, and a wash basin or some other container to hold the solvent during the cleaning process. Before you start dry cleaning, be sure to vacuum the rug thoroughly on both sides.

Because solvents are highly inflammable, be sure to open windows for proper ventilation. Don't do your cleaning near a fire or other open flame —and better not smoke either, then you can be certain that you are free from all danger.

HOW TO USE THE SOLVENTS

Fill wash basin about half full with solvent (about three pints) and have at least two Turkish towels handy. Saturate one towel in the basin, then squeeze as dry as possible. It is important not to work with a very wet towel, since only the surface of the rug is to be cleaned, and the burlap on hooked rugs is best left dry. Using the damp towel, start at one end of the rug, and work across one row at a time, rubbing in all directions. As each row is cleaned with the saturated towel, follow immediately with the dry towel, rubbing the surface of the entire row in the same manner. Never start a new row until the previous one is finished. If and when the solvent becomes cloudy, dump it out and use some fresh mixture—also use a clean towel whenever this seems necessary. It may take you about ten minutes to clean a large hooked rug. When you are through, allow the rug to dry thoroughly before using.

While you are at it, you may as well clean all your hooked rugs. The task is amply repaid as you see the lovely colors of the pattern emerge as you work. Cleaning as recommended will not harm any fabric and you will find that, if anything, your rugs will improve with age when proper care is taken. Never shake a hooked rug violently or beat it outdoors, as this will shorten its life more than any normal hard wear.

SPRAYING WITH MOTH PREVENTIVES

After dry cleaning your rugs, they should be sprayed on both sides with a reputable moth spray. Use only the best brands and apply spray according to directions on the container. Although the vacuum cleaner does its share to make moths feel unwelcome, a good spraying will clinch the deal.

CLEANING WITH SOAPY LATHERS

Although, personally, the author prefers the dry cleaning method described above, there are many specially prepared soapflakes on the market which can be used for cleaning fine fabrics in rugs and upholstery. Suds are made in hot or warm water, and the idea is to transfer soapy foam to a small part of the rug—perhaps 20 square inches—at a time, and using a small flat brush to scrub the foam-covered area gently. Immediately follow this operation by rubbing off the soapy foam with a damp towel, rinsing it in warm clear water in-between times, and wringing it dry. Use just as little moisture as possible, remembering that it's the foam rather than the soapy-water solution which makes this type of cleaning successful. Cover entire surface, cleaning just a small space at a time. Allow the rug to dry thoroughly before replacing in the room, and follow cleaning with moth spray.

CLEANING WITH DRY POWDERS

There are also several dry powders on the market specially made for rug cleaning. These are sprinkled over the surface of the rug, and are then swept off with the vacuum cleaner. These powders should be used with extreme caution, since they have a tendency to dull the colors of the rug.

TO PREVENT RUGS FROM SLIDING

As a precaution against accidents, small rugs can be anchored by placing nonskid pads underneath them. These may be all rubber, or if you prefer, you can now get rug cushions that are rubberized on just one side. Another alternative is to sew rubber jar rings underneath the corners of the rug. This helps to some extent, but is not as effective as a rubber pad. If you have a rug at the foot of a stairs, better tack it down if no nonskid pad is used underneath. Small holes left in the floor from small carpet tacks may always be filled with a wood filler, should the rug be removed.

REPAIRING DAMAGED SPOTS IN A HOOKED RUG

To mend a damaged spot, such as a burn or a tear, remove sufficient loops around this spot so that a small new piece of burlap can be sewed underneath the main burlap. The patch should reach at least one or more inches beyond the damage, and be machine stitched. Hook this space again, matching the neighboring work as nearly as possible. Use as many strips as you can from those that were removed.

STORING HANDMADE RUGS

A hooked rug should never be folded when it is stored since folding puts a strain on the tension of the hooked burlap. Instead always roll the rug, preferably with the right side out. Braided rugs should also be rolled when stored.

30
MARKETING RUGS

After making several rugs, the hooker is not only a more experienced worker, but a more ambitious one too. It is then that one of the most pleasant avocations may easily become a vocation. Rugs are an expensive item to buy, but, being a necessary part of every home's furnishings, there is a constant market for them. A spare-time hobby can thus be developed into a successful little business.

Most hookers enjoy their work and have little idea of selling a rug while they are engaged in its making. But as each pattern is finished the hooker is always challenged to do another rug, this time the "perfect one!" The collection increases and the time eventually comes when, to make room for the favorites, the hooker is prepared to let one or two of the earlier rugs go if a buyer can be found. Whether this is the manner in which you find yourself in business or whether it is your intention from the beginning to hook for your daily bread, or some of it at least, the moment comes when you need to find an outlet for your rugs. How then to set about it?

To most of us, the first thought connected with selling anything is to advertise it in a newspaper. This is certainly one way to bring your handiwork to the public's attention, particularly if there is a local newspaper with a classified advertisement section. A small notice may cost only a dollar or two and bring you in contact with a private buyer or a retail store with ready customers. In the latter case you will not of course get the full price your rug is worth, for stores are in business, too, and have to take a considerable mark-up. Frequently, also, a customer answering such an advertisement seems to expect some kind of bargain. The thing to do is to stand firm on the price you have in mind, remembering that there are people who will pay any reasonable price for a rug they particularly admire, and you must, if necessary, bide your time until you are able to make a satisfactory sale. You will then find that one sale leads to another as people start talking about your work in the neighborhood. Of course, if you are selling your first rugs, which may not, for one reason or another, be quite up to professional standard, it would be unwise to hold out for too high a price, as that would be a sure way of killing the goose before it laid the golden egg.

Even though none of your friends may be a prospective customer, one of them may know of someone who would be, so if you are ready to sell a rug, it never hurts to let your acquaintances know, for sooner or later they may have just the right contact. Nine chances out of ten you will find a buyer this way, providing the work is up to marketable standard.

With a few exceptions, antique dealers like both hooked and braided rugs, especially in early designs which make a perfect accompaniment to the finest American antiques and reproductions. While your local antique dealer may not be in a position to buy your rug outright, it is more than likely that he will be glad to have you leave it on consignment, at an agreed net price to you when a sale is made. Your chances of making a sale in the right price bracket are greater in reputable outlets of this type than, for instance, in a general furniture store that features home furnishings at standard or cut-rate prices. People search out antique dealers for "one-of-a-kind" pieces, and the discriminating buyer is usually ready to pay more for just the rug he or she has been looking for. So by all means try your best local antique dealer and get a signed receipt with the price he agrees to pay you when the rug is sold. Unless you are short of ready cash it is better to leave work on consignment than to force a quick sale by lowering your price below the sum the rug should fetch. If you happen to be an antique collector yourself, you might try some sort of an exchange deal on your rug with the antique shop. This has sometimes proved a way of getting a rug on display in a store, and the subsequent sale has resulted in made-to-order rugs for the same client. You may be sure that if one rug sells quickly in your local store, there will be many more orders waiting for you if you want to take them.

If you don't have an antique shop in the locality, there may be a good restaurant that would be glad to display your rugs and sell them as a sideline. In summer colonies there are often craft centers and gift shops that make a point of displaying handicrafts, so check your possibilities there, too.

Interior decorators are also in the market for rugs. These professionals are called upon by clients to furnish rooms either in homes or public buildings in a particular style or color scheme, and it is possible that their budget permits a high price for a rug hooked or braided in a special design or color. If you are prepared to make rugs to order, a letter addressed to a number of interior decorators listed in your classified telephone book—or some national directory, may very likely bring you a contact worth following up.

Sometimes these decorators, like the antique shops, are prepared to take a rug on consignment so they can get orders for similar types of designs from their customers—or they may sell the rug directly from the floor. Never neglect any opportunity to have your work on display, for this is the best way of developing a steady market.

Check up on local art and craft exhibits so you can get one or more rugs entered. Even local fairs may provide you with an opportunity to get your rugs in front of the public, and there is always a chance of winning a prize and getting a notice, perhaps an illustration, of your work in the local papers. One success like this will more than likely lead to others on a bigger scale. If your designs are unusual, it is worth having a group of rugs photographed and sending prints to the editors of craft magazines or the national home furnishing magazines with a letter asking them if they would be interested in featuring them in an article. Editors are always on the lookout for unusual designs that are in good taste. Any such publicity is good for building up your home industry.

Yet another way to develop your business is to have your local printer or stationer print up a card or folder, showing one or more illustrations of your rugs, together with an announcement of an exhibit at your home, or else a general notice advertising that you have rugs for sale. This could be sent to names in the local telephone directory—or to dealers in the yellow pages of the classified section in a city—or to any other list of potential customers that may be available to you.

PLANNING SALABLE HOOKED RUGS

Now that several ways of developing a market for your homemade rugs have been suggested, it is important to stress the execution of designs that have sales appeal in the expensive range. Study the trends and preferences of present-day furnishings in a tour of home furnishing exhibits in the larger and better stores, or by scanning the leading home furnishing, fasnion, and art magazines. If you are most interested in certain period designs, try to visit the museums for authentic patterns that can be copied. It is often better to specialize in one type of rug which appeals to you most, and build your reputation around this style.

There is always a good market for the early American type of rug in a simple design, for this will go with almost any popular informal room setting. There is also a growing demand for simple modern designs of an abstract nature for the modern room. This field so far has been relatively neglected by the rug hooker. It can honestly be said, however, that designs of any period, tastefully adapted, will find a market with one or another type of customer, and that poor designs of any period or inharmoniously colored rugs will always lose out in the quality market. Give plenty of time, therefore, to the study of designs and color combinations featured in the museums and the best national magazines, in other home furnishings such as wallpapers, draperies, chinaware, needlework, as suggested earlier. And if you have a particular flair for designing, don't be afraid to experiment. Tasteful originality is the greatest asset of all in the long run.

As for practical sizes and shapes, the 3-by-5-foot rug is perhaps the most popular, whether oblong or oval. A 4-by-6-foot rug is often too large for the average fireplace, though it may fit elsewhere in a room. Round rugs are not as popular with most people, but can be most effective in certain specific settings. For a larger rug, 6 by 9 is a popular size for an oblong hooked rug, or an oval braided one. Larger sizes are best not attempted except on specific order.

Last but not least in planning salable rugs, choose colors with care. Remember that neutral backgrounds are best, for they will go with most color schemes. This doesn't necessarily mean borders should be neutral too, for a rather dark color will emphasize the central design, frame it effectively, and provide a practical edge for wear. Green or brown is a popular seller here, and dark gray, dark blue, or black are close runners up. However, an all-black background is not generally a good seller, though a few people may select it. The color of the border should harmonize with the colors used in the center of the rug. Muted tones are always a better general choice than vivid colors, though the latter can be used in limited quantity for color accents. Don't use large areas of bright colors and don't mix vivid greens or blues with candy-colored pinks or quantities of other artificial-looking colors; if you do the rug is sure to look cheap. Follow natural colors found in flowers, foliage, grasses, or grains for harmonious and restful effect.

VALUE OF HOOKED RUGS

It is very difficult to place a proper value on hooked rugs, as much depends on the size, the design, the coloring, the quality of material used, the type and quality of hooking, also the type of buyer for whom the rug is intended. What is worth a great deal to one person may have little appeal to another.

Usually a fine, smooth, evenly hooked rug with subtle shadings has a much higher rating than a coarsely hooked piece finished in a fraction of the time. Similarly a rug in practical muted colorings with a restrained and tasteful design will bring a better price than a hastily conceived or splashy design. Choice woolens used in hooking will also enhance the value, for a rug thus made looks better, is thicker, and will wear for a life-time and longer. All these points must be taken into account when placing a value on the handmade rug.

The author can only generalize when stating that the value of rugs can vary from around $4.00 to $15.00 per square foot, depending on the rating it can be given on an aesthetic and craftsmanship basis.

Anything from $45.00 to $100 might be a fair price for a well-made 3-by-5-foot rug. If exceptionally good in design, materials, and technique, yours may be worth more, particularly as you become well known in the field.

The author sold some of her early rugs for a very low price, but later on received three figure sums for 3-by-5-foot rugs, and recently the same just for the loan of small hooked pictures measuring 17 by 26 inches to be reproduced on greeting cards. In the final analysis, what it really boils down to is how clever can you become at making your rugs irresistible? Better price them on the low side to begin with and gradually raise the price as the demand for your work increases. Check the prices on comparable pieces in antique shops and consult with your friends and dealer. Remember that well-designed and well-made rugs will fetch much higher prices than the average pieces hung en masse at roadside stands. As in starting any other business, you must feel your way until your reputation is firmly established.

31

TEACHING RUG HOOKING

Teaching rug hooking is almost as much fun as making rugs. One of the principal reasons for this is the friendly enthusiasm that prevails at such groups. Most students will admit that class day is one of the pleasantest of the week. And strangely enough, no one learns more than the teacher in these classes. It doesn't matter how experienced he or she may be, beginners are always popping out with different ideas—and good ones, too!

A wise teacher doesn't force any personal preferences on those who are learning, but instead, tries to help each one to carry out original ideas. Most ruggers have favorite colors and at least a general idea of what they are striving for in their rugs. Because of inexperience, however, they need help in developing technique. The teacher's job is to see that a pupil's rug as nearly as possible suits the personality of the maker, just as a good interior decorator carries out a client's preferences in furnishing a home.

The first step in teaching, of course, is to make sure that everyone in the class knows the correct technique of hooking—how to hold the hook properly, pulling through the end of a strip, then how the loops are made. As in every other craft, the right beginning means so much. All teachers have seen new pupils try to do hooking with their burlap so loose on the frame that every loop was pulled through with extreme difficulty. The importance of attaching the burlap to the frame so that it is "drum tight" should be demonstrated. The beginner doesn't realize that this will make hooking twice as easy unless the difference is clearly shown. Another tendency to watch out for is the novice's tendency to cut strips too thick. Even though you say ⅛ inch, they nearly always come up with wider strips, and then, of course, have difficulty pulling them through the burlap. You must also see that they understand about keeping the strip straight and untwisted underneath the design. Don't underestimate the importance of great emphasis on these so-called "small points." As to holding the hook, show them your method, but let them find the way that seems easiest for them. Only if proper progress is not being made should you encourage them to change to a different method of working.

It should be unnecessary for the teacher to do any hooking on the beginner's rug, except at the very start when demonstrating the *hooking technique*. While some teachers do believe in hooking a petal now and then, the author believes the beginner perfectly capable of executing her own shading if properly instructed. Then too, such attention will usually take too much time away from the rest of the class. Everyone learns best by experience, and mistakes can always be corrected afterward if necessary.

One of the most successful ways of illustrating shading is the *crayon method*. For this purpose the teacher must have complete assortment of crayons. The kind used for kindergarten work is fine. This simplifies shading so that the beginner readily understands. For this purpose, the author uses yellow crayon to denote highlights, which is where we begin in flower making. Any light color crayon can serve the same purpose. Then use black or another dark-colored crayon to designate the shadowing in the flower. This is usually enough, for the new hooker should be able to develop the in-between shades of a flower thus outlined. However, if additional help is requested, you can use an in-between color, such as a red or green crayon mark, to show how the color series is worked. This may be necessary to illustrate the blending of a rose, as this flower is the most difficult of all to do successfully, probably because it has no center like the daisy, for instance, or stamens like the jonquil or lily.

Some instructors have better success in teaching when each member of the class is making the same pattern. In this way everyone concentrates on one particular flower (or other design) at a time and has the opportunity of comparing results. This is a wonderful idea for a short time, but soon some hookers will be ready to start a new flower while others are still in the middle of doing the first one. Since, in the author's opinion, it isn't fair to hold back those who are speedier, it therefore becomes necessary to let the fast workers go ahead.

Blackboard instructions are a wonderful way to illustrate the shading of flowers. Take the rose, for instance. This can be perfectly illustrated on the blackboard so that even the beginner will grasp the technique of careful shading. It is usually an excellent idea to illustrate a different flower or other design in detail on each class day, allowing the hookers to make their own adaptations. Let the class suggest what they most want illustrated the following week or class day so you have time to prepare the material and can help them in their immediate needs. If you find drawing on the blackboard difficult, a drawing prepared beforehand can be pinned up for everyone to study.

Encourage each member immediately to start their scrapbook on the shading of various flowers. Then as the blackboard illustrations are done, notations may be added to the book for future use. Explain fully the benefit of the scrapbook as a ready source of inspiration. All kinds of designs and photographs that appeal to the individual student should be cut from magazines and other sources for constant reference on outlines and shadings.

Nothing helps the morale of a class like a beautiful hooked rug on display. Every rug class should have one or more at each session, for it adds no small amount of enthusiasm and zest to the entire group. There's a lesson for everyone in each type of hooked rug if they observe everything about it closely. It may be the way a certain leaf curls, or the center of a daisy, the detail of the scroll, the manner in which the background is done, how different patterned woolens look when hooked, and so on. A general evaluation of the rug displayed is good class practice. Guest rugs are nearly always available as most everyone is happy enough to have others see their work.

While you may start your class hooking simple designs with ready materials, you will soon need to demonstrate the dyeing process. And the quicker you can break down the average person's resistance to this work, the better. Like so many other things, it isn't difficult once a person knows how. So let the class watch you dye a color series, and then make experiments of their own at home. With fears about dyeing dispelled, you will find your class coming up with many original color combinations from which everyone can benefit.

Choice and arrangement of color is of primary importance. Most members of a group will have had little or no experience with planning colors, and may rely on you for guidance here. Get a color chart or color wheel if you can (there are many illustrated in books on color, flower arrangement, interior decorating and allied subjects) or make up one yourself, so that everyone may study the relationship of colors—the primary colors, contrasting colors, complementary colors. Then show your own scrapbook containing actual illustrations which have been worked out harmoniously by artists, decorators, illustrators, needleworkers, as a guide to color schemes and groupings. This way the class will learn what colors go best together, how to balance colors over an entire design, so that there isn't a predominance of blue in one corner, for instance, red in another, yellow in another.

The student will soon grasp the idea of color balance, but you will find that many are then likely first to divide a chosen set of colors equally all over the rug. This may be right for block patterns and sometimes for hit-or-miss designs, but in groups of flowers in the center of a rug an exactly even distribution of color would, of course, look unnatural. In other words, you must demonstrate that color balance doesn't necessarily mean a red flower in the center, a blue one placed evenly at either side and at top and bottom, a yellow one in each of the four corners, symmetrically arranged. Some teachers find a good method of demonstrating this point is to arrange a colorful vase of flowers in which the principles of color harmony and balance are demonstrated. The study of prize-winning massed flower arrangements, flower prints, and paintings will be helpful to the student both in matters of color and design.

Beginners also need advice about choosing appropriate patterns. Explain first how hooked rugs should be designed to tie in with the furnishings of a room. Formal rugs are right for certain interiors, such as Georgian and Victorian, and informal designs for Early American. Most rooms represent a mixture of furnishings, but the general atmosphere will be one of formality or informality. A good guiding principle in this case is to take a cue from the wallpaper, draperies, chair or sofa coverings, or a picture on the wall, so that the rug has some relationship both in style and color to other featured objects in the room.

It is also most important that good designs of each style be found, for a student may hook beautifully, but if the design is in poor taste she will never be able to sell the rug successfully should she want to. Encourage students to visit rug exhibits of other classes, museums, study needlework heirlooms, the better furnishing magazines for styles, patterns, and colors. In later classes, after all general instructions have been given, begin classes by giving each student personal help for a few minutes, starting with the first to arrive and on through the last. When the entire group has had a chance to ask individual questions, start again with the first, allowing equal time all down the line, checking on what each has done and discussing further shading. In groups larger than twelve, each may have to receive less individual attention, but this usually works out satisfactorily too, for with more people working, the class has greater variation of material for purposes of comparison, and the more expert students can often help the others out and profit themselves by studying fellow workers' problems.

Some rug teachers report they find the "constructive criticism" method an extremely beneficial way to begin each class period. In this way some time is spent by the group in discussing each design as every member of the class shows his or her work. Even though some students are shy at first about displaying their rugs, when they become used to it, they find the discussions invaluable in turning up new ideas and points on hooking various details.

As to the question of tuition fees, several teachers known to the author have charged from $1.50 to $2.00 per person for a four-hour class of five to eight pupils.

Part II

F O R E W O R D

To a great many people, hooking and braiding are ways of life so fascinating and rewarding that they are no longer classified merely as hobbies. This is good, for even in this space age everyone benefits from pursuing a creative art. In today's increasingly informal decors, hooked or braided rugs play an important part. They are such a sure way of glamorizing a home that it is no wonder that more new homemakers are turning to hooking and braiding than ever before.

Hooking is an art that talks about you, and given half a chance it can say some very complimentary things. This book is planned to help you to design, create, and enjoy priceless items that are truly yours.

First, you learn selectivity and discrimination as applied to patterns, color, and workmanship. You will find the book easy to understand and the directions simple, as many teachers who adapted the first edition for their classrooms have proclaimed. Part II brings *Rug Hooking and Braiding* completely up to date, with absolutely none of the original book deleted. Thus, we offer two books in one.

Ideas, methods, and short cuts learned over years of practice are shared with you. I hope you will read our two books in one for fun, as well as for help, and that it will enrich the lives of you, your family, and all your friends.

After having read the book, use it as a springboard to incorporating your own ideas at their best. It is then that you will deserve the compliments that your work is sure to bring.

DOROTHY LAWLESS

32

CURRENT TRENDS

Florals of traditional design retain their popularity, perhaps because we are a nation of flower lovers. But because of their suitability to dining areas, as well as their natural appeal, fruit designs are also popular, whether in rugs on the floor, in chair seats, or in pictures. Some other perennial favorites are trains, eagles, rural scenes, mallard ducks, dogs, and cats, just to name a few.

Geometrics have a timeless appeal, of course, giving endless opportunity for expressing individual preferences in design and color. We offer an unusual geometric which is sure to add more than its share of charm, besides being the ideal way of using your odds and ends. We call it "Friendship 7" and assure you it is a must.

Of particular appeal in picture making is the use of decorator burlap as a base on which only the design is hooked. On red, aqua, yellow, gold, green, or even natural color burlap, chosen to suit the decor, simple, uncluttered designs assume a third dimension. Plain, unworked burlap provides the perfect mat for a wide shadowbox frame of light wood. Aside from their unique charm and popular appeal for one's own home, hooked pictures provide the perfect gift for a wedding, birthday, Christmas, or any special occasion. Of no less importance to the maker, such pictures can be completed in just a fraction of the time usually consumed for hooking those with a background.

The return of the rocker gives the rugger many an opportunity for self-expression. Especially different is the hooked headboard. A good design source is Eaton, the famous designer of stencils for the Boston rocker of the past. If the chair is painted, the background of the headboard can be the same color as the chair. When attached with tiny headless nails, the headboard looks like a painted stencil.

Hooking has branched out into many other new fields, such as handbags, totebags, headboards for beds, bedspreads, lamp shades, samplers, afghans, book covers, table tops for under glass, coasters, doilies, silhouettes, miniature pads for table legs, and even corsages!

There's a new soft brown-red color called "barn red" that has proved a great favorite with many, especially on the West Coast. It is easily achieved by dyeing any bright red material with a light brown dye bath, simmering for permanency. We first used this color as a background in a room-size fruit rug, where it provided the perfect setting for realistic fruits, such as pears, peaches, strawberries, and melons. Now, after much use, we can vouch for its practical qualities as well. So if you have maple or other light-wood furnishings, we assure you of the pleasing compatibility of barn red.

33

HOW TO TRANSFER YOUR
PATTERNS MORE EASILY

The crinoline or organdy method of pattern transfer is one of the easiest and surest. Simply trace off your design on either crinoline or organdy, then pin the cloth drawing in the right position on burlap. With an ink marker, available in stationery stores, draw over the lines of the pattern. The ink will go through the cloth and your pattern will be clearly marked on the burlap.

Another way is to use hot iron transfer pencils as a means of transferring designs. This method is not as reliable, however, since the pattern tends to be unclear unless you really bear down with the pencil before ironing.

If you use carbon paper for tracing, you will find it more successful to place a sheet of glass between table and burlap as a base over which to draw. The glass makes a much harder surface than wood, and lines therefore tend to be sharper.

Still another method is to make pin pricks on your paper pattern and then transfer the pattern onto burlap by sponging over the design with an inked sponge. This will make an almost solid line if the pin pricks are close enough together.

A more time-consuming, but fairly easy, method is to make a stencil of your design. With a stencil knife, cut slots for the lines of your design on heavy, stiff paper made for that purpose, using a sheet of glass as a base on which to work. Both stencil knife and paper are available at stationery stores and hobby shops. As in the pin-prick method, the slots should be placed closely enough together to make an almost solid line. Place the stencil on the burlap and go over it with an inked squeegee roller or sponge. Since this method does take so much time, it is most practical when the stencil is to be used more than once.

34

THE "FRIENDSHIP 7" HIT-OR-MISS RUG—A MUST

Because the author was working on this rug when Colonel John H. Glenn, Jr., made his historic space flight, she called it "Friendship 7." Friends then viewing its progress volunteered contributions—a special plaid or another pretty mixture that they thought would look good.

"Friendship 7" makes an ideal hall runner or area rug, and for a carpet it is perfect. A more handsome rug you can't imagine, and what's more, you are never handicapped by a shortage of material, since it is an ideal way to utilize those odds and ends that every rugger accumulates.

You can complete the canvas design in a few moments by accurately marking off 7-inch squares on whatever size burlap you wish. Using a long ruler, pencil off the lines first, then go over the lines with an ink marker, so that they will remain clear throughout the hooking process.

Lightly mark off emphasis lines with crayons first, then, when their arrangement is satisfactory, ink them in. Alternate the directions of the lines in each block.

Now comes the time to organize for work by sorting all your odds and ends of woolens. Place all the reds in one big plastic bag, the blues in another, and so forth until all the woolens are separated. Group them according to color rather than intensity or shade of color. Place the plaids with their predominating color. This organization is imperative, especially if the rug is to be room size.

Blocks	Emphasis Lines
1. Green	Brown
2. Yellow	Khaki
3. Blue	Dark blue
4. Dull dark red	Tan
5. Tan	Brown check
6. Soft red	Wine
7. Gray	Coral
8. Lavender	Dark brown
9. Blue	Dark blue
10. Yellow and light rust	Brown check
11. Green	Brown
12. Light pink	Black
13. Soft red with some gray	Rose
14. Lavender	Purple
15. Tan and brown tweed	Brown
16. Gray	Yellow
17. Yellow and gold	Brown tweed
18. Blue tweed	Dark blue
19. Pink and gray	Black
20. Light green	Dark green

Note: For a larger rug or carpet, the above order may be repeated exactly or slightly varied. You may change the colors to fit your supply of woolens.

Begin the hooking by separating the blocks with a single row of brown or black. Before hooking the emphasis lines or filling in the blocks, however, they must be carefully planned. For even though the finished rug projects a casual air, each of the strong emphasis lines within the blocks must be precisely placed and the colors carefully thought out.

See fig. 91 for a suggested color arrangement. If you make your own arrangement, pin slips of paper to each block to designate its particular coloring. While preplanning is necessary in this rug, don't hesitate to change your mind every so often if you decide another color would be more pleasing. The emphasis lines can be the darkest or the lightest shade of the material used to complete the block, or they can be contrasting colors, as coral or yellow lines dashed across a gray block, or brown lines through a lavender block. Dark lines through a block made with plaid material make an attractive square. In "Friendship 7" many different plaids were incorporated and, more often than not, they formed the prettiest blocks in the rug.

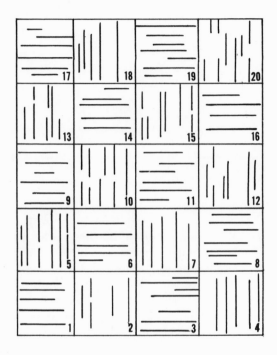

Fig. 91. "Friendship 7." Made up of 7-inch blocks, easily mapped off on any size canvas, this is not an ordinary block pattern, and it is much more attractive than the usual hit-or-miss rug, with which it shouldn't be confused. Emphasis lines in alternate directions provide a different approach to the casual rug. It's a hit-or-miss that's hard to beat!

35

WHAT ABOUT COLOR?

Color has been defined as what you see when you first enter a room. One noted specialist, who has designed everything from automobiles to supermarkets, says No to the question, Do Americans know how to use color? But whether or not this is true, they seem to do a very good job of it.

Decorating authorities now advocate the use of more coloring than ever before. Current magazines more often than not show warm red backgrounds combined with blue and white or other decors equally dramatic.

We hear of color versus emotion: Red is associated with cheerfulness, defiance, and power; black suggests despondency; brown, protection; purple, dignity; yellow, cheerfulness. Do colors have certain emotional meanings to you? Certainly it behooves people to surround themselves with compatible colors.

Manner of living has a bearing on color choice too. Homespun colors with warm, friendly appeal may appear garish in a formal decor. The trend for informal furnishings now calls for more color. Colorful hooked and braided rugs are not only suited but almost a necessity to those who know the difference they can make in a home.

Carpet manufacturers suggest new bold trends for area rugs. We agree that area rugs are important and should be imaginative, vibrant, and even emotional in treatment. They unite the furnishings and social elements of the room. Seating arrangements can be unified and framed with harmonious area rugs.

Never before have we had so many colors and types of dyes from which to choose. And to many, the dyeing is quite as intriguing as working up the colors. Should all pieces in the same color match? Definitely not, say experts. Actually, this is undesirable and seldom possible. Because various materials take dye differently, they can't always be color matched. However, they can be dyed to blend. Slight variations between dye lots is unavoidable even in commercially dyed fabrics, so don't be exacting when repeating colors.

Choosing soil-resistant colors is often as much a matter of geographical location as of practical taste. In the South, where the earth is a warm, coppery color, woody beige tones may least likely show soil. Other places have gray soil, while still others have brown loam. Therefore, practically speaking, these factors should be considered, especially in suburban or rural areas where there is an increasing trend toward outdoor living.

Some people claim that light colors darken with age, others that they grow lighter. With today's efficient vacuum cleaners and other methods of cleaning, light colors need no longer be shunned. However, we suggest that you select rug colors that are more intense than you prefer, because in time they do soften, which shouldn't be confused with fading. Of course, they should never be unduly exposed to the sun.

Artificial light changes colors, so, when making your selections, do also consider the effect of lamp light. If possible, avoid those colors which appear muddy at night under artificial light.

36

HOOKING PRETTIER ROSES

In another part of this book, there are directions for hooking a simplified rose. The purpose of the following outline is to show you how to make the rose appear more natural. The first step, of course, is to assemble six or more suitable shadings, ranging from light to dark, and we do mean dark unless you wish to make a pastel rose.

A natural fluffy look can be achieved by occasionally breaking the shadow lines of the rose. For instance, you can break the shadow surrounding the rose bowl by letting it extend as a curved line toward the tip of a petal, as a separation between two petals. Then, continue the shadow a couple of loops away from the curve. The bowl of the rose will still look full and round, but will be all the more enhanced by such shadow breaks in a couple of places. The shadow breaks themselves will appear more realistic when made in two or three rows which taper off toward the edges. If a line consists of 3 or 4 loops, carry an additional, shorter line underneath, thus breaking the single-line effect.

Make some of the petals darker than others, shading them in the same way as the lighter ones. Make occasional turnbacks on the petals even though none are indicated on the design. These are done in the same manner as leaf turnbacks.

The bowl of the rose should be the lightest part, the heart of the rose the darkest. A good rule to follow is to make the lower third of the heart the darkest shade. Many prefer the top petals slightly darker. Always use intermediary shades for filling in those small leftover places in the rose.

37

COLORINGS FOR VARIOUS FRUITS, FLOWERS, AND FOLIAGE

FRUITS

Green Apples. The green apple with a red cheek requires spot dyeing with bronze green over yellow material for most of the apple. For the red cheek, overdye yellow wool with just a bit of scarlet or apricot dye. If you prefer using swatches (color series), the green apple may be done from either a bronze-green swatch of very soft colorings or a bright green swatch.

Blackberries. Blackberries require only 3 colors: black, purple, and some light blue or pink. The latter colors provide highlights and should be done last.

Cantaloupes. The cantaloupe cut, if showing, appears delightfully realistic done in talisman rose shadings or apricot. The rind of the cantaloupe is best done in various tweedy mixtures, with cool green strips separating sections of melon rind. Or, if you use a swatch (color series), bronze golds also produce excellent realism.

Currants. These need 3 shades of bright red, dyed from cardinal over cream-colored material.

Seedless Grapes. For pale green seedless grapes, use a swatch shading from white into soft, pale silver green. The grape stems look most natural in a color resembling tan shoe leather.

Peaches. Make realistic hooked peaches by shading from swatches of buttercup into talisman rose. The two colors blend beautifully for making the transition from yellows into pinky tones for the blush of a peach.

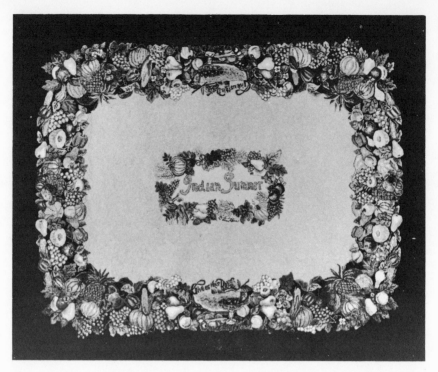

(Photo: John Carlson)

Designed and made by the author, the completed dining-room rug "Indian Summer" features a sampler idea, with the wording at the center of each side border. It was made in the room where it is now used.

Pineapples. The pineapple requires pale chartreuse material spot dyed with cardinal, bright green or bronze green, and golden brown. This will necessitate 3 steps in the spot-dyeing process. (See chapter 15 for directions on how to spot dye.) In addition you will need some light yellow and gold strips. The spot dyeing should result in a blending of shades rather than any strong shades. When hooking, be sure to make one part of the fruit more shadowed than the other. You may use red tones to provide shadowing at the top of the fruit. This will be a nice contrast to the green foliage above the pineapple. Begin the pineapple with dark brown crisscrosses of diamonds, using a lighter brown at the edges. For the light side of the fruit, use dark rust dots in the diamond centers. Fill in the diamonds with light chartreuse and gold shades, using the lightest color at the center, surrounding the rust dots. Another way is to use a combination of soft green-golds and chartreuse. For the dark side of the pineapple, use red-brown within the dark brown diamond outline, follow with green-golds, and finish with light yellows and golds against the center dot.

Watermelon Slices. The watermelon slice is charming among other fruits. Turkey red dye makes the perfect shade—the red color gives a luscious ripe appearance. You also need white and a pale cool green for the cut edge, plus a variety of greens for the rind, if it shows. For seeds, use a small black-and-white or brown-and-white check material.

FLOWERS

Calla Lilies. Calla lilies are pretty shaded from white into beiges and soft browns instead of the usual pale grays or greens. Dye the swatch from brown dye. Allow for some pale creamy yellows in the white of the calla lily.

Daisies. For white daisies, dye a swatch using a very small amount of black dye. One shade should be pure white. (See chapter 13 for dyeing directions.) Colors so dyed are of soft violet tones and may be preferred to the usual grays. A pretty center for such daisies can be produced from a brown-and-white check material spot dyed with gold and outlined with the same check material spot dyed with Nile green. Used with white, a small amount of navy or dark blue is also good for dyeing material for daisy petals. Centers made from plaids are great favorites.

Pansies. For a different pansy, try the white rose swatch in all its series, plus straight mahogany as the darkest shade for the pansy whiskers. Another pansy variation is to make a yellow bottom petal, with 2 adjoining petals in sky blue, and the top 2 petals in turquoise.

(Photo: John Carlson)

This is how the designing proceeded for "Indian Summer," a room-size rug.

Illustrations that inspired the pattern called "Indian Summer."

FOLIAGE

Acorns. Acorns usually need a dark brown outline for both the crowns and the nuts. Fill in the crowns with a tiny brown-and-white check mixture. You may range from light into dark in the nut part, using either tans or bronze greens.

Oak Leaves. An oak leaf with colors ranging from mahogany to rust complements nearby pine needles of pinky rusts or copper tones. A leaf shaded from green into gold complements yellow needles nearby.

Pine Cones. About 3 or 4 shades of spice and a brown shade is all you need for pretty cones. Shade each little section from light at top to dark at base if the cone is tipped downward, and vice versa if tipped upward. This will create the effect of light falling on the cone. Occasionally, rusts add interest among other pine-cone colorings. Another idea is to range from chartreuse, yellow, and rust into darker browns. Chartreuse highlights with olive greens or yellow highlights with golds and browns are also effective colors for pine cones.

Pine Needles. You may use all the greens, from the lightest to the darkest shades. When hooking, alternate with chartreuse, bronze golds, soft yellows, pinks, dark olive greens, blue-greens, bronze greens, and mauve and lavender colorings.

38

SHADING LEAVES

SHADING THE AUTUMN MAPLE OR OAK LEAF
FROM A ONE-COLOR SWATCH

While spot dyeing has been recommended for autumn leaves, a different but realistic effect can be obtained from using a one-color series. Ways to use the series may vary, but a favorite way is to begin with the lightest shade directly against a brown vein at the center, and finger in the following shades in the series, making the leaf darkest at the edge. You may then outline the tip in shade 4. Use a darker shade, say, 5, at the middle edge and use 6 to complete the lower part of the leaf. Another way is to make one side of the leaf darker than the other; for example, use shades 1, 2, and 3 for one side and 4, 5, and 6 for the other. Outline the leaves in appropriate shades. The edges of the leaves may exactly match the adjoining parts, or they may be slightly lighter or darker. Turnbacks in tan, chartreuse, or a contrasting color are pretty.

SHADING OAK LEAVES BY COMBINING
DIFFERENT COLOR SWATCHES

It's fun to vary leaves by using 2 or 3 different colors. For instance, start with dark bronze green for the base of a leaf, change to the lightest green toward the middle, and then finger in light yellows or pale golds. A blending of the lightest shades make the most pleasing transitions from one color to another. In blending red and green, for example, finger pale pinky red into pale green. Soft shades of salmon, apricot, or gold blend beautifully into about any of the light greens.

It may be wise to omit some of the darker or stronger shades when using the 2- or 3-color combinations for leaves. For colors for leaves, consider gold, bronze green, blue-green, gray-green, rust cardinal, talisman rose, salmon, peach, apricot, copper, golden brown, mahogany, mummy brown, mulberry, maroon, and mustard green. At every opportunity study real autumn leaves for greater inspiration. Even though nature surpasses you, it's always thrilling to paint gaily colored leaves with one's woolens.

SEVEN WAYS TO SHADE LEAVES (fig. 92)

(The lightest shade is represented by 1, the darkest by 6.)

A. Make the tip of the leaf the lightest shade, gradually going into the darkest shade at the base.
B. Begin with 2 at the tip, shading into 1, 2, and 3 on one side of the leaf and 3, 4, and 5 on the other, and finishing with 6 at the base.
C. Make the tip shade 3, and continue with 1 against center vein and through center part of leaf. Shade out from the center with 2 and 3 on both sides and use 4 for the base of one side, 3 for the other.
D. Use 4 at tip, continuing with 5 and 6 on one side and 1, 2, 3, and 4 on the other side.
E. Use 5 for the tip, and follow with 4, 3, and 5 for one side and 4, 5, and 6 for the other.
F. Make the tip shade 6 and continue with 5, 4, 3, and 1 on one side, and 5, 4, 3, 2, and 1 on the other.
G. Use 1 and 2 for leaf turnback on the tip of the upper right side. Use 2, 3, and 4 on the opposite half of the leaf. Complete the side that has the turnback with 5 and 6 only, using the darkest shade next to the turnback for contrast.

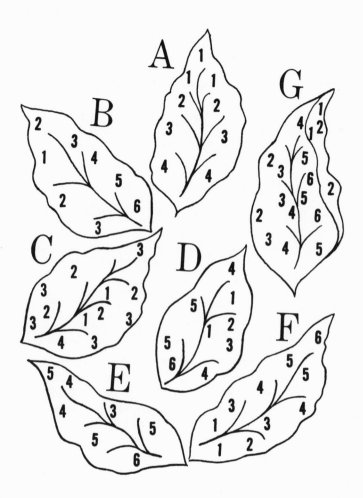

Fig. 92. Seven ways to shade leaves.

39

HOW SATISFACTORY IS
AUTOMATIC
WASHING-MACHINE DYEING?

Washing-machine dyeing has both advantages and limitations. The main advantage is the convenience of dyeing greater quantities at a time, more evenly than by hand and with less difficulty. In addition, wools are more thoroughly rinsed in a washing machine, and there are no messes to clean up. How nice to have no dye on one's hands!

As for limitations, it stands to reason that with no boiling or simmering, the dark, rich coloring is never quite achieved when dyeing over light colors, and colorfastness is somewhat questionable. But to intensify a coloring for backgrounds, as in darkening or dyeing any of the pastel shades, machine dyeing works very nicely.

Dissolve the dye in boiling water in a pan and thoroughly mix before adding it to the machine. Then let the washer fill with very hot water to a low or medium level, according to the amount of material to be dyed. The medium level should handle perhaps 4 pounds of wool. Before adding the wool, it is best to wet it thoroughly in warm water and then squeeze it out. The wool is thus immediately receptive to the dye bath. Stir the wool thoroughly in the dye bath and then add ½ cup of plain (uniodized) salt. Be sure to set the machine for modern fabrics. Allow 2 or more 12-minute agitating periods. Continue using the same dye water, switching the dial for the longer period at the end of each 12-minute period. After the wool has rinsed, fluff dry it and hang it in the air to complete drying. No ironing is necessary.

Washing-machine dyeing is good for changing undesirable tans, grays, or other such shades, especially if they are faded or streaked, into more attractive colors. Pink dye warms up dull grays. Brown dye intensifies or softens a great many colors.

Your washing machine may also be used to soften a too-intense color for a background or border. One or more sudsings in a detergent will remove much of an over-bright shade, as red, green, or purple. Process material as for washing, and set the dial for modern fabrics.

Instead of washing out a bright color, you may soften brighter shades by overdyeing with khaki, gray, black, or a color that is a direct contrast to that being softened. As an example, a bit of red will soften a garish green, and some orange dye will change purple into a pretty brown.

Lest you dread using your machine in dyeing, for fear of the job of cleaning it up afterward, I hasten to add that this is the least of one's worries. A bit of detergent swished over it with a damp cloth and a final rinse quickly restores its original condition.

40

COAT-HANGER DYEING

The origin of coat-hanger dyeing is uncertain. This method was demonstrated to the author in one of her classes. To begin, tack the ends of six strips of wool on a wooden coat hanger. Any light colors can be used. Soak the strips in a detergent and then in boiling water to which ½ cup of any kind of vinegar has been added. This can be done best in a long, shallow pan, preferably enamel.

Dissolve 1 tablespoon of bronze-green dye in the water and quickly dip all the strips in the dye bath. Squeeze out the excess liquid. The top of the strips will come out lighter than the rest.

Add 1 tablespoon of Nile-green dye to the same water, and again add vinegar. Dye just the lower quarter of the strips in this dye bath, just long enough to pick up the dye, but not long enough to set the color, as this is done later. Add silver green or silver gray-green dye for dyeing the lower half of the strips over the previously dyed ends. Use plum, mulberry, or purple dye for dyeing almost to the top of the strips. Remove the strips from the coat hanger.

Now for setting the color. Do not rinse the strips; wrap them together in aluminum foil and roll them up lengthwise, or fold them crosswise. Steam them for 30 minutes in simmering water, which must not cover the rolls. This fully sets the various colorings. Then thoroughly rinse the dyed strips in clear water and hang to dry. The results should be a beautiful blending of colors suggesting innumerable uses.

This kind of dyeing is suggested especially for scrolls where colors are related yet afford interesting contrasts. Leaf scrolls are very nice in the softly blended greens. You are sure to find many uses for such greens, for most ruggers never have too much of this color.

41

NEW WAY TO SPOT DYE
BY ROLLING MATERIAL

First saturate 3 or 4 long strips in water and wring them out. Stretch each strip flat across a newspaper. Using a different color dye for each section of about 10 inches in length, sprinkle dry dye on the strips, not too heavily yet enough to show dark in patches. (Thus you may have 2, 3, or 4 different colors for each strip, depending on its length.) The amount of dye needed depends on the thickness of the wool, heavier wool obviously requiring more dye than thinner wool. Overlap the different dyes slightly. Roll up the damp, sprinkled strips individually and let them set for 15 minutes. Then place them in shallow boiling salted water. A shallow enamel pan or a wash basin can be used. Let the rolls simmer for about 5 minutes, then turn them and let them continue to simmer for another 5 minutes. Sprinkle them with additional salt as they simmer, adding hot water as needed. Never permit the water to cover the material. Finish by rinsing the strips thoroughly and letting them dry. The results are exquisite colorings that are blended as though painted on with a brush. Colors should intermix and overlap yet retain much individuality in each section. For those who otherwise have difficulty in spot dyeing this is an easy way to get very satisfactory results. Suitable materials for spot dyeing are outlined in chapter 15, where you will also find another excellent method of spot dyeing.

The roll method of dyeing described here is especially suitable for autumn leaves or certain fruits. It can also be useful for scrolls where a soft change from one coloring to another is desired.

42

PAINTBRUSH DYEING

Ruggers may find paintbrush dyeing easier and perhaps less messy than certain other methods. Certainly it provides a wide variety of shades suitable for all manner of hooking. Any kind of wool can be used, but light colors are suggested. Results will depend on the type of wool, its color, and the dye. Choose the dye colors as you would for spot dyeing. For autumn leaves or peaches, for example, use apricot, gold, and bronze green. Mix each dye separately in a jar allowing 1 teaspoonful of dry dye to 1 cup of boiling water. This amount of dye for each of 3 colors will be good for as many as 6 strips of wool approximately 3 inches wide by 15 to 20 inches long. Use a separate, small, clean paintbrush for each color, so that the dyes won't intermingle. Don't leave the paintbrushes in the jars while dyeing.

First wash the wool in a detergent, making it receptive to dye, and do not rinse. Begin painting at the end of the strip, using a different color for each ⅓ of its length. Colors should begin dark, gradually growing lighter through that particular coloring. The last color used should darken toward the strip end. Let the colors overlap slightly for a blended effect. These overlapping areas blend even better if you smooth them with a clean brush dipped in warm water.

To set the colors, place a few sheets of paper toweling in a flat, shallow pan (preferably enamel) and then lay 3 strips of wool side by side over the paper. Add enough water and white vinegar in equal amounts so that the liquid is about level with the top of the strips, but not above. Use no salt for paintbrush dyeing.

Bring the liquid to a boil and then simmer the strips until the water clears. Add a second layer on top of the first after it is processed. As the vinegar water boils down, add more of equal proportions, always keeping the solution to the level of the top strips. Add other layers, repeating the process as before, until all the strips are in the bath. The top layer is always the lightest shade with those below becoming darker. Simmer 20 to 30 minutes, depending on the weight of the material. Use tongs for handling wools. Rinse the dyed strips in warm water. The strips should now be a wide array of shades suitable for various flowers, leaves, and fruits. Varying shades of a single color may also be dyed in this manner. Many say that paintbrush dyeing is not only a guaranteed method of producing graduating shades but that it is also easier than many other methods.

43

CONTINUITY DYEING

This differs entirely from previously described dyeing methods. Certainly it is both easy and effective. Formula 1 produces even blendings of a single color all on one strip. Formula 2 produces two or more color changes, where one color so blends into the adjoining one that it is impossible to tell exactly where one ends and the next begins. Thus, for example, on a very long strip, shadings may change from white into yellow, then pink, and finish off with lavender-gray shading into darker gray.

FORMULA 1

Soak the strip of wool (approximately 4 by 36 inches) and wring it out. Dissolve dry dye, using about 1 teaspoonful for a 36-inch strip, by pouring 1 cup of boiling water over the dye. Add the dissolved dye to 4 cups of hot water in a shallow pan over low heat, and stir. Place a 6-inch end of the strip in the dye bath. Stir and add a tablespoonful, or more, of salt. Simmer for 2 or 3 minutes and then push an additional 6 inches of the strip into the dye bath and let it simmer for a short time. Repeat this procedure with each additional 6-inch section of the strip until the entire strip is dyed. Do not remove the sections from the bath until the whole strip is dyed. While dyeing the strip, it is most convenient to hold the undyed part of the strip in your left hand, leaving your right hand free to add salt occasionally and to stir.

Proceed with the dyeing carefully, always watching the results so as to determine better the amount of time you should allow for each step. The ideally dyed strip begins very dark, then changes to an intermediate shade,

236

and ends with a very nearly white color. If you have used white as a basic color, the end should actually be white. This type of dyed strip is well suited to flowers, leaves, fruits, scrolls, etc. To use, cut through the strip lengthwise. Make longer strips for scrolls and shorter strips for hooking flowers and leaves so that the entire range of shadings on the strip will be used.

FORMULA 2

Use a long strip, as in Formula 1, or 5 or 6 short strips of varied colors, such as light green, gold, yellow, beige, pink, and gray. The strips should be about 5 inches wide. This is a good way of utilizing odds and ends.

Again, the first part of the strip should be kept in the dye solution as you proceed with the following sections. However, use only about ½ as much dye as you did for Formula 1. One-half teaspoonful is approximately enough, depending on the weight of the wool and the color of the dye. Use more dye for dark colors and less for lightweight materials. To begin, put ½ of each strip in shallow water over heat, crushing it into a wrinkled pile with a fork or tongs. Hold the remaining part of the strip in your left hand. Sprinkle dry purple dye over the crushed, wet wool to obtain uneven tones. Then add salt and stir gently a few times, but only enough to make sure that dyed parts aren't overly dark in certain spots, since the dye is sprinkled directly over the material. Simmer for a few moments until the water clears, adding more water if necessary.

Repeat this process with the second half of each strip, but this time use sky-blue dye instead of purple dye. After simmering the strips, remove them and rinse them thoroughly first in warm water and then in cool water.

It is always exciting at this point to examine the results, since each time they may differ according to the materials used. You have been successful if the colors blend as they vary, and show interesting highlights of the original dye color.

Formula 2 is recommended for hooking such flowers and fruits as irises, pansies, morning glories, plums, and grapes. In plums and grapes, for instance, strips dyed by this method contain good shades for highlights, such as pink among blues and purples. Visualize, also, irises with dark purple lower petals and pink and light blue tones in the upper petals.

In an experiment, garnet dye was used at the beginning of the strips over gold, beige, and pink wool, and was followed by jade-green dye as a second section color. The ends were left undyed. As can be seen, a greatly varied color arrangement is possible to suit almost any purpose. It's a very good idea to make notes as you go, for you may want to repeat the results. Such an array of different hues can afford much exciting hooking, as well as unusually good realism.

44

THE CONTINUITY-DYEING
METHOD FOR FLOWERS

YELLOW ROSES

In no other way than by continuity dyeing can one achieve such unusual and delightful yellow roses. Of course, the resulting strips can be used for other hooking purposes, too.

Method 1. In general, follow directions for Formula 2, above, using dark brown dye for the first half of the strip. (Don't try to measure the dye, since the required amount depends on the size of the strip, but use it sparingly.) However, instead of dyeing all of each half at the same time, dye about ⅓ of the strip with the brown dye bath, and gradually push in a little more of the strip at a time until about ½ of the strip is dyed. This should consume all the brown dye. Now add a generous sprinkling of dry yellow dye and dye the remainder of the strip in the same manner along with the first half.

Satisfactory results are easily achieved, and this is the way it works. The brown dye, added first, has an influence over the remaining coloring even as the yellow enhances the brown coloring. Thus, the entire long strip should be the lightest of yellows at one end, changing gradually into lovely warmer yellows, then soft bronze browns, and finally darker brown. Can't you just imagine what beautiful yellow roses this will make?

Method 2. Instead of brown dye use purple, but continue with yellow dye, as in Method 1. The resulting strips range from yellows into browns again, but the browns have a slightly red cast because of the purple dye.

TALISMAN ROSES

Use mulberry dye for the first section and continue with yellow dye as for yellow roses, again following Formula 2. The resulting strip ranges from clear yellows into tawny soft red-brown colors, and finally into rust reds which have a faint tinge of lavender, exactly like that seen in talisman roses. When hooking the rose, add to this color range some creamy white for highlights, as well as a darker brown for shadowing if greater contrast is desired.

WHITE FLOWERS

Use white material and gray dye, which will form the darkest end of the strip, shade 6. Before the water clears, add more of the strip for shade 5. When the water has cleared, add a bit of purple dye to produce shade 4. With the water now cleared again, add a little pink dye for shade 3. For shade 2, add a little gold dye. Leave some of the end of the strip undyed for shade 1. This makes a beautifully blended strip from white and creamy yellow into a pink, and then lavender as it finally darkens into gray. Imagine apple blossoms, or dogwood, or hibiscus with such subtle shadings.

45

HOW TO HOOK WITH
CONTINUITY-DYED STRIPS

Continuity-dyed strips are generally cut length-wise, but if crosswise cutting seems easier for shading, it's perfectly all right to cut them so. With patience and ingenuity, there is no limit to the possibilities for the application of continuity-dyed strips. Don't hesitate to create your own methods of using this type of dyed strip.

LEAVES

You will especially find continuity-dyed greens for leaves a great advantage and time saver in both dyeing and hooking. A long strip may begin with the darkest green and continue gradually into a creamy green. Start the leaf with the darkest part of the strip at the base of one side. Hook up to the tip on one side and then from the tip to the base on the other. This will create a leaf that is darkest at the base on one side and lightest at the base on the other side; each side will gradually work into the medium shade at the tip. Although leaves are usually hooked in short, slanting rows following the direction of the veins, as explained elsewhere, either of these methods make pretty leaves.

IRISES

For the upper petal of an iris, use the very lightest end of a strip combined with white for highlights. The shades may range from light to medium blue. Use dark purple for the center veins. For the lower petals, use shades of purple, ranging from light to dark, with the darkest again used for petal veining. Complete the flower by allowing the lighter shades to fall amid the darker veining, with the medium shades making up the petal tips, except where they overlap. Contrast here is essential so that the petals will stand out from one another.

46

BACKGROUND, SCROLL, AND
BORDER TALK

BACKGROUNDS AND BORDERS

Beautiful and unusual backgrounds and borders are often discovered by trial and error. In fruit and autumn leaf designs, brown, the true autumn color, is an excellent foil. A very pretty border was dyed from 2 packages of brown dye combined with ½ teaspoonful of cardinal for 3½ pounds of various beige wools. Home dyeing produces uneven coloring, which further enhances the border coloring.

An attractive border of antique black was produced from ½ teaspoonful of olive green dye plus 1 teaspoonful of black dye over bright Kelly green wools. This was dyed in a washing machine. A lovely green-blue background was produced from equal parts of réséda green and dark blue dye over pale green wool. This also was dyed in a washing machine. Another background was done from an old white-and-pastel plaid blanket, overdyed with silver green dye. The resulting background resembled a wavy, water-color painting.

A pretty dark green border was made from forest green dye over gray woolens, allowing one package of dye for each pound of wool. For the author's pattern called "Glamor Rug," which features irises across each end, a mauve-rose background was combined with a dark mahogany border. So great was its success that it has been copied dozens of times. The materials for the rug were dyed as follows: For the mauve-rose color, 2 packages of garnet dye combined with 1 of cardinal, plus a scant teaspoonful of black dye, was used to overdye a soft beige mixture. For the mahogany-brown border, a full-sized beige coat was overdyed with a combination of 1 brown, 3 cardinal, 2 garnet, and 1 black packages of dye. The scroll within the border was merely an outline of silver green. This focused attention on the handsome floral center.

A pretty rose-colored background can be obtained from using 2 parts of old rose dye to 1 part of dusty rose over light gray material.

While the above ideas are outstanding, it is suggested that you do your best to procure background and border colors without dyeing whenever possible. Never before have there been available so many handsome materials, or so many shops specializing in rugmakers' needs. Recommended are the now popular muted checks and other such mixtures that just miss the solid-color classification. These provide a pleasant change from the plainness of the past. They appear in various pastels such as pinks, blues, grays, and creamy yellows, and are a new approach to background hooking.

HOW TO ESTIMATE THE REQUIRED AMOUNT
OF WOOL FOR BACKGROUNDS

This problem can be solved in either of two ways. The first is simply to allow ½ pound of wool for each square foot of background. The second way is to spread the unhooked wool three to four thicknesses deep over the background on the pattern. Three thicknesses of heavy material may equal four thicknesses of thinner wool, so use your judgment. This method may be somewhat simplified by dividing the material into four equal parts, then checking to determine if one-quarter of it will cover one-quarter of the rug area.

SCROLLS

Scrolls can be done in a variety of ways and colors. There are many new kinds of mixtures, plaids, and checks that make outstanding scrolls. As previously mentioned, entire scrolls may be done without thought of special outlining or shading techniques. Colors may be gay, for they become much softer and blended when hooked. They should, however, repeat the predominant coloring of the rug.

Red plaids are recommended for scrolls, and even better, for the veining of scrolls. The over-all effect is usually softened by whatever color is used adjacent to the red.

If a plaid contains too much white, a short dyeing with a yellow dye will change it into a charming mustard-toned mixture. In fact, a bit of yellow dye will make all the colors found in plaids softer and prettier. Reds are turned into brick tones and blues into blue-greens, dark grays become a dark mustard color and light grays dye into a lighter mustard. These grays make especially charming scroll colorings. The plaids in general become nearly as neutral as the favorite gold scrolls and yet have a twentieth-century sparkle. However, be sure to make the background and border a plain color when using such mixtures for scrolls.

Brown-and-beige or brown-and-white checks make pretty narrow scrolls when used against plain beige backgrounds or solid brown borders. With today's streamlining of everything, it isn't surprising that scrolls are simplified, and often even eliminated. As previously mentioned, scrolls are often merely outlined to contrast with the border color, which is used to fill in the scroll.

THE PAINTED SCROLL

The basis of the painted scroll is continuity dyeing, explained in chapter 43. You can change the shading on a painted scroll as quickly as if you were actually using a paintbrush. Suppose we make a 2-toned scroll with a gray background and a dark blue border. The scroll should be divided into units, some of which will be muted rose tones, but most of which will be silver greens. The greens may be dyed over either a faded green or a soft gray or beige. Each gives a different effect. Garnet dye over dull green or gray material produces the dark rose shades. Light green wool overdyed with rose is used for the lighter rose shades.

The technique for applying the 2-color idea is important, yet simple. In fact, it is easier than making the regular 5-shaded scroll. The strips of wool may be 6 or 8 inches wide by about 3 feet long. Dye them carefully, following the directions given for continuity dyeing on page 237, so that the shades graduate from dark to very light. Allow perhaps as many as six steps, or units, as the complete strip shades from one extreme to another.

Each unit of the scroll will have its own strip. Opposite units should be done to match, more or less. Cut through the strip lengthwise so that one end of each scroll unit will be very light and gradually change to very dark at the opposite end. In this way, outline and fill in each unit.

In wider scrolls you may use a strong contrasting color for the center veins, which may then be enhanced with graduating greens on one side, and shades of pink graduating into rose on the opposite side. This produces a painted effect.

ADD SPARKLE WITH PLAIDS AND OTHER MIXTURES

A wider use of plaids as scrolls, borders, or even backgrounds is well worth consideration. Even gay plaids completely lose their overly bright colors when hooked.

Some plaids with much white are improved by being lightly dyed in yellow, pale green, or other pastel, according to your over-all color scheme. Yellow is the author's favorite overdye since it always produces a prettier plaid for scrolls or other special work.

The effect of a plaid border is similar to that of tweed carpeting, except for its different colors. For the informal decor, such colorings are quite in order. However, it may be unwise to use a plaid border directly against a fancy scroll or a floral design where overbusy effects should be avoided. Plaids must adjoin solid coloring to look their best.

In a scroll, a plaid of colorings that relate to the other part of the rug can be a very pleasing change. Beginners are especially happy with plaids, since their shading problems disappear. Since the right plaid is not always available, it's a good idea to keep on the lookout for desirable plaids and other good mixtures.

For leaf veins or floral centers a choice of plaids is essential. The gayer ones are desirable for floral centers, while the muted ones of darker coloring are very often perfect for leaf veining, spirals, stems, etc.

47

SIGNATURES AND DATES

Be sure to sign and date your hooked pieces—it may be more important than you think. Signatures and dates are always hooked in, of course. Before starting to hook, pencil in the outline of your name and the date to be sure they are pleasingly placed. In a picture, the signature generally appears in either the right or left lower corner, depending on which part lends itself best. In a rug, your signature should be an integral part of the design. Omit just enough of the design to squeeze in a legible signature. If your name is long, you may hook in just the first initial and the last name, or, if it is unusually long, you may use just initials.

The date of completion should be placed somewhere near the signature. The last two digits of the year with an apostrophe are preferable to the four—for instance '62 instead of 1962.

A spot-dyed strip is very good for hooking signature and date. Use dark shades on light backgrounds and vice versa. A plaid or other mixture is also pretty. A single row of hooking is sufficient for both the signature and the date.

48

HOOKING A BEDSPREAD

Although this is seldom done, it is fun, and not too much work, since only the design need be hooked. Unlike rugs, an open pattern is best. White or cream monk's cloth in single- or double-ply weight is ideal. If you prefer a pastel or stronger color background, the material can always be dyed if not otherwise available, but your basic color must be colorfast.

What design is suitable? This is a personal decision. Flower-lovers may choose a floral center grouping, perhaps encircled with a narrow ribbon with a bow and streamers. An older chenille bedspread may provide just such a pattern, or another of equal charm, and you can hook the design in single rows, in the same manner as the original design. Another idea is a crisscross design over the entire spread, with a few center flowers. Perhaps a geometric design, in the form of outlines only, taken from some of the handmade quilts, would interest you. An eagle in the center is suitable for certain period rooms where the style is traditional and the colors are red, white, and blue.

Whatever the pattern, do keep it simple and uncomplicated, and keep your hooking to a minimum so that the spread will be a practical light weight.

49

IDEAS FOR PICTURE HOOKING

If it were generally known how easy picture hooking is, everyone would be rushing to make one. Even beginners surprise themselves.

Many picture-makers prefer either very few or no cut ends on the top side. The effect is a sharper picture and is best for the detail required in portraits. The use of only jersey for picture hooking has been tried with great success. Using only commercially dyed jerseys, a beginner did the Currier and Ives "Spring Blossoms" with excellent results.

TREES AND FOLIAGE

Soft brown tweeds for barren tree tips produce fernlike branches, avoiding too blunt an ending of branches. These tweeds are also good for tree trunks, producing snowy effects.

Green checks and tweed mixtures make summer foliage and trees easy to do. These can be dyed over basic checks of brown or black and white. Use dyes of both cool and warm greens for the various greens necessary. A blue-green tree may contrast nicely with an adjoining one in bronze green.

To make billowy and realistic tree foliage, make semicircles with the lightest shade of a 6-shade swatch throughout the tree top. Proceed with all the shades, working downward. Use intermediate shades of green to fill spaces between completed semicircles.

A hooked picture designed from the Currier and Ives print "Little Snow-bird."

FARAWAY HILLS

These must be a more neutral color than grassy lawns in the foreground. Pale bronze greens can be used to create the effect of distance where less variation of color is required.

DISTANT MOUNTAINS

These are effective in 3 or 4 shades of mauve. They may either darken or lighten toward the horizon, depending on the picture. Always add shadow lines as necessary. Never fill in hills, mountains, or skies with straight lines, but rather use wavy or slightly curved lines.

WINTER SCENES

Winter scenes are definitely the easiest types of scenes to do. Metallic mixtures in the snow make a glistening effect. Protect the white snow when filling in by pinning a piece of cloth over the hooked work. Should the work become soiled, however, a dry cleaning will restore its beauty.

Rivers in winter scenes are good in cool blue-greens with little bronze green, except for reflections of sunsets or such, where touches of gold, too, provide greater realism. Series of shades may be advisable for water scenes. You may taper off a stream of water in the distance by using darker, narrower curves. Shade winter ponds with teal blue combined with much white for the ice and snow. Add light highlights such as off-whites, light blues, and light grays for a greater icelike effect.

SUNSETS

These vary as much in pictures as in life. For instance, an all-yellow sky or a blue sky above a yellow sunset can be lovely. Mahogany-colored mountains are delightful against a yellow sky.

PORTRAIT PAINTING IN WOOLS

It's fun to create closeups of children, such as those in the Currier and Ives prints "Little Lizzie," "Little Snowbird," and "Little Blossom." Tastes have recently turned also to the simple and primitive designs seen in some oils. These are all the more charming when hooked, and not too difficult for anyone with hooking experience, providing a good color picture is used as a guide.

FACIAL FEATURES

Begin hooking facial features with a single dark outline above each eye. Continue with a bit of blue and black for the eye pupils, and complete the

1956   LITTLE BLOSSOM

(Photo: John Carlson)

The mate to "Little Snowbird," this hooked picture was adapted from the Currier and Ives print "Little Blossom."

eyes by hooking a dot of white at corners. Make eyebrows short, curved lines of cocoa brown. The mouth is made from a soft pinky red wool. For the face itself, begin with rosy cheeks and change to a soft petal pink for the remainder of the face. Use 3 or 4 shades of brown or gold for the hair, making the part in the hair the same as the face color. Divide the face and neck with a shadow line of faint cocoa.

MOLDING THE FINE DETAILS

One means of greater perfection in picture-making is to use fine scissor points to mold the finer details. After hooking, push and mold the finished loop to your heart's desire with the scissors, held points down. Minimize as necessary or spread out certain details for importance and realism. In this way you perfect each part as it is pushed and shaped into place. This is especially necessary for facial detail. You may be surprised to discover that your work is far better than you originally thought, after going over it with your scissor points.

PICTURE FRAMES

The wide frame is a must for providing balance to the texture of a hooked picture. Frames too large for a picture may be cut down to size, or the picture can be enlarged. To do this, add to the picture a strip of velvet wide enough to fit the frame. The velvet should first be sewed to the burlap from reverse side so that the stitches do not show from the front. Its color may blend or contrast with that of the picture. A strip of flannel instead of velvet can be charming if the frame is of pine or maple. Another idea is to hook the colored band around the picture. This band may be an inch wide for small pictures and up to 2 inches wide for a larger picture.

Natural wood frames are now in fashion. Oftentimes they are available for finishing as desired. The old 3-part frames, often coated with plaster of Paris, make ideal frames for hooked pictures, but require much patience and labor to restore to their natural wood. Their mellow tone, however, is never found in new wood.

A trio of hooked birds makes an
attractive grouping.

(Photo: John Carlson)

50

MAKING A HOOKED SAMPLER

One of the author's students had a lot of fun
working out a personalized sampler in class. The design was a room interior, with fireplace, dog, cat, and even grandma in her rocking chair,
which added whimsy to the scene.

Being a sentimentalist, the student went a step further in personaliz-
ing her sampler for framing. A tall wooden clock on the mantel was done
from her memory of one that had belonged to her family. Grandpa was
done as an enlarged picture on one side of the mantel, balanced on the
opposite side with a pair of silhouettes depicting her two grandchildren.

Even the family dog was in the sampler. All this detail was done by an
amateur at hooking, though, of course, a very adroit one. Results were
truly a family sampler to be cherished. So admired were the results of this
young grandmother that her eight-year-old grandchild tried her hand at it
and was rewarded by a blue ribbon at the Los Angeles County Fair the following summer. Just another proof of how a favorite hobby catches on,
with far-reaching effects.

51

THE RIGHT WAY TO SHOW OFF
YOUR SCENIC RUG

There are right and wrong ways of using the scenic rug, and the wrong way may account for certain objections to scenics on the floor. But, if a rug is properly placed, surely the most discriminating person could offer little objection. We must admit that care should be taken, however.

Much is said about the focal point of the room, which is very often a hearth. However, a bay window or a picture window may be your focal point. Either the hearth or window makes the perfect place in front of which to place your prettiest scenic rug. It is here that your callers will see it first. But more important, it will be viewed rather than trampled on. It can even set the mood of the room. Can't you just imagine a winter scene that suits the outside weather? Or a green countryside scene that just spells spring and summer? A friend of the author uses her "One Horse Shay" scenic rug in place of a Christmas tree before the fireplace with its mantel appropriately decorated for the holidays.

Not everyone has scenic rugs for such occasions, but it is a rather good idea to have two or three different scenics so that the mood of the room can be changed every once in a while. A bay window provides a perfect offset position for a scenic rug, where it can be used with a table and chair grouping. Lay the rug against the table but not underneath. In a picture window, use the rug in the same way. This definitely makes an important center of interest.

Many ruggers like to add a personal touch to their scenics, such as a mailbox with their name or street. But the scenic rug should include less detail than a picture. The design should be simple, in keeping with a rug. Unsuited as floor pieces are wildlife, the American eagle, and closeups of people.

52

WAYS OF HANDLING
A ROOM-SIZE RUG

Different sizes of lap frames are helpful in handling a room-size rug. Begin your hooking in the center of the rug and keep the outside part folded or rolled and pinned, so it will be out of the way as much as possible. Lap frames can vary in size according to need, since they are easily acquired or put together.

Frames of 3 different sizes are most convenient. One, 13 by 30 inches, proves ideal for longer stretches of border settings. Another, 20 by 20 inches, is a good choice for the deeper parts through the center. A third, 13 by 19 inches, is handy for catching smaller leftover parts where the larger frame would have been awkward.

If the room-size rug is occasionally steam-pressed on its back side as it grows, it is more pliable and easier to control as the work continues. Too, it looks so handsome that it encourages one to carry on.

Another way to handle a room-size rug is to hook it in two 40-inch or 48-inch sections, depending on its width, but leaving a comfortable margin on the inside edges, so that the sections can be easily sewn together just before the center section is hooked. It is wise to have the burlap basted together when you transfer the design to it to make sure the design matches. Then you can take it apart until you complete each strip to within 2 or 3 inches from the edge. At this point, sew it together again, and finish hooking through the center. In this way, you will have to work with the large whole rug as little as possible.

A third way to handle the room-size rug is to use a specially made frame, sufficiently long to carry the complete width of the pattern. One rugmaker got the cooperation of her husband in making a 20-inch by 12-foot frame. Four wooden horses supported the frame. Her pattern of a block design, required the frame to accommodate 2 rows of blocks for each setting. Bolts were used to fasten wooden supports on the frame as necessary. The bolts were easily released for shifting the pattern. The hooked part of the rug was kept rolled up in back of the frame where leather straps had been attached for holding the roll.

53

PEPPING UP AN OLDER RUG
OR CHAIR SEAT

With a few changes, it's amazing how pretty older pieces become. First, of course, vacuuming and dry cleaning are in order. But then study the design to see what needs redoing. Faded flowers with little personality are well worth changing into fresh new flowers—perhaps by fingering in the wool instead of shading by more ordinary methods. Drab roses may be so brightened that you will gladly add new leaves.

Such changes do take a little time, but only a fraction of that required in making a big rug or a complete chair seat, for the chances are that the background is still very good. You are really bringing the older pieces up to date. White roses on a chair seat made a few years ago were changed into glowing red roses with new mossy green leaves, all against the original pink jersey background. With the little effort of changing two roses and a few leaves, the hooked chair seat is like new.

Sometimes just a few floral changes in an older rug do the trick, making the rug look newer. Even a more interesting scroll may enhance your rug. Sometimes a gay plaid for filling in the scroll part adds untold charm. A whole background was once changed when a transition was made from formal to informal decor. While this seems like a lot of work, it is far less than doing a completely new rug and thus takes far less time. Simple touch-ups such as outlining a flower or leaf often enhance an older rug. Autumn leaves can be beautifully freshened by stronger outlines. White daises or other such flowers are quickly renewed with new fluffy white wool petals or a new floral plaid center.

54

CARE OF RUGS

GENERAL CARE

Everyone knows the vacuum cleaner's value, but do you know that a thorough vacuuming consists of 7 strokes over one area, 4 forward and 3 in reverse? A light cleaning calls for 3 strokes, 2 forward and 1 in reverse. At least one thorough cleaning and additional light cleanings each week are recommended. Make a habit of vacuuming the backs of your rugs every 6 months. Never wash valued hooked rugs in a washing machine, for obvious reasons. Never use soap or alkaline solutions, nor ammonia, water softeners, washing soda, or other such cleaning preparations.

For a general cleaning, dry cleaning is still preferred, as cleaning solvents do not harm colors or fabrics. If you use a synthetic detergent, use 1 ounce to 1 gallon of water, and lightly sponge the surface—never soak the rug. Rub briskly with a soft, dry cloth.

There are many ways of prolonging the life and beauty of our delicately constructed hooked rugs, which are often exposed to rugged service. A closet near the back door for rubbers, work shoes, and perhaps children's play clothes saves wading through a bedroom. In bad weather, it's wise to cover rugs near doorways. Keeping floors waxed and polished helps keep rugs clean too. Gas or oil furnaces are recommended for cleaner heat. We must pay for the luxury of a fireplace by vacuuming more often, although fire screens offer good protection from much of the soot and ashes.

Place rugs so that chairs won't scoop the edges as they are moved. Glass cups and metal casters on chairs can make indentations in your rugs; metal casters are especially harmful since they can also cause iron rust. Rubber cups are by far the best since they are quite harmless.

Rugs should be turned around periodically, for more evenly distributed wear, and protruding ends clipped as soon as they are obvious. Be sure to rebind any worn edges before they become overly worn. To prevent permanent indentations, move your heavy furniture every so often, but be sure to lift it rather than drag it, or you may damage the rug texture. When vacuuming small rugs, run the vacuum cleaner diagonally across them and off the edges so that the suction won't lift or roll the rug. Air conditioner humidifying devices help overcome dry air, which is hard on rugs.

REMOVAL OF SPOTS AND STAINS

Accidental stains need immediate attention while they are still wet. Use a clean cloth or tissue to absorb as much of a spilled liquid as possible. Old powder puffs, freshly laundered, make excellent spot-cleaning pads. Each type of stain requires different treatment. Here's a mild, effective, and harmless formula for general spot removing: To ½ pint of lukewarm water, add 1 teaspoonful of neutral (nonalkaline) soapless detergent—the kind used for delicate fabrics. Mix until clear. Apply mixture directly on the stain with an eyedropper. Sponge the area with a clean cloth, starting at the outer edge and working inward, to avoid enlarging the spot. With another clean cloth, dampened with warm water, sponge the area again. Don't rub vigorously, as this causes surface distortion, worse than the stain.

Grease spots not responding to ordinary dry-cleaning methods may disappear if a combination of corn meal and salt is rubbed over the spot with a brush, and the spot is then vacuumed.

WAYS TO REMOVE SPECIAL SPOTS AND STAINS

Chewing gum, milk, grease, or butter: Gently rub spot with carbon tetrachloride; never use soap or detergent (soapless cleaner).

Coffee, candy, sugar, ice cream: Rub gently with warm water and detergent.

Fruit juices and acid substances: After blotting with a wet cloth, dilute 1 tablespoon baking powder or ammonia in a quart of water. Apply this solution and in a minute blot up and repeat.

Ink, cocktails, candle drippings, rust, or iodine: These stains call for professional cleaning.

Pet accidents: Blot up soiled spot. Dilute 1 cup white vinegar in a quart of water. Saturate spot and let stand. Blot up and repeat, finishing with a soapless cleaner and blotting as dry as possible.

Blood: Wipe with a dry cloth, then with a wet cloth, using cold water.

MOTH PREVENTIVES

There are many fine moth repellents on the market, in the form of crystals and sprays. Plastic bags are the answer for storing rugs and they give full protection if tightly fastened. A rug in daily use and vacuum cleaned often needs no special spray. When storing a rug, it is wise to spray both sides before placing it in a plastic bag. Store in a dry place. The plastic bag will fully protect rug from dust and air, as well as from moths.

55

WHAT'S NEW IN BRAIDING

CHENILLE RUGS

For a perfect washable bathroom or kitchen rug, try braiding one with chenille. This is a wonderful way of utilizing old chenille bedspreads and bathrobes. Many especially like the all-white chenille rug. Or, if you prefer pastel colors, just collect basic chenilles of desired colors. Old turkish towels work nicely for additional material.

Chenille rugs are braided in the usual way, except that you needn't do any basting ahead of time because the cotton strips are more easily controlled than woolens. You just fold as you braid. Tear strips about 3 inches wide for average braiding and sew the ends together on the bias. You may lace the braids together with linen thread or nylon hosiery (see page 263 for directions), which many claim is easier on the hands.

BRAIDED COVERS FOR FOOTSTOOLS

Covers for footstools and the so-called milkstools with three legs are now very popular. These covers are usually cupped like a hood around the edge and are usually left on as a permanent part of the stool. Begin a cover for a round stool as you would a round rug, with the color scheme planned in advance. First braid and lace a flat covering the size of the stool top. Then for the next 2 rows or so, depending on the thickness of the stool, lace the braiding more tightly, so that the edge is boxed. The cover must now be matched carefully to the stool so it will fit well. Proceed with the lacing, with the cover now on the stool, so that the next row is cupped underneath the top. This means that the braiding will again become tighter. Thus, the stool top is completed and securely finished off.

If you wish the cover to fit more securely, let the final row of braid go behind each leg, but otherwise lace the braid tightly just below the stool top. If you have any difficulty in getting the cover to fit you can always take out the lacing, as necessary, and relace. Braided hoods are fun to make and make very charming additions to stools. They often make the perfect gift and can be completed in a short time from odds and ends left over from braiding.

BRAIDED COILED CHAIR OR STOOL SEATS

These twisted candy-stripe stool tops are thicker than usual, since they are coiled sideways. This extra thickness provides a padlike seat. The author's color scheme for a coil seat is as follows: Make a small red center, changing into a combination of red, white, and plaid for the next four rows. Then, continue with a plaid combined with blue for the next 3 rows. Then add a row of red and 2 rows of white. Three rows of red complete the pad.

This type of seat should not be laced but stitched. Take short stitches at the beginning of the coil and take longer ones as the coiled seat grows so that the completed piece will lie flat. The colors should change at the same part of the turn each time, unless you prefer a hit-or-miss effect. When your coiled seat is the size desired, finish it off by tucking the ends underneath, within the finished braided cables. This makes a flat coiled top which doesn't cup over the edge or tuck underneath.

You are sure to be delighted with your coiled seat pad, for it, too, can be completed in a short time and can be made from leftovers. It is reversible too. It can be used on a round top stool attached with tiny headless nails, and it is equally attractive for a chair or rocker pad, presenting an entirely different design from the usual braided seat pad that is laced.

Seat pads braided and laced in the usual way are, perhaps, preferable for a set of dining chairs since they are more easily matched. The coil seat, mentioned above, is more of a novelty, or conversation piece, and it might prove a bit more difficult to make a matched set.

56

PRACTICAL POINTERS
ON BRAIDING

Braided rugs are at an all time height of popularity, and just about everyone can use at least one. Interest in braiding is often prompted by the fact that woolens that can't be used for hooking because of weave or color can be used for braiding. These practical, reversible rugs are also extremely adaptable, since they can be enlarged, if necessary, after indefinite usage. Muted colors will tone down any overly bright colors you may wish to use when enlarging a rug.

PLAIDS AND OTHER MIXTURES

Mixtures are a must in braiding. Nothing so enhances the great charm of braided rugs as these mixtures that soften and blend the whole rug. Use some of the mixtures right at the beginning of your rug, as well as using them often throughout the rug. If you prefer a closer blending of colors than is available in your mixtures, a slight dye bath of the predominating colors may be the answer. This may be done over any of the neutral mixtures, such as brown-and-white or black-and-white tweeds or checks. Even plaids may be made to blend better after being given a dye bath suiting your color scheme. Little or no dyeing may be necessary if you use care in accumulating your braiding materials. One of the author's rugs is called a "rummage-sale rug" since nothing in it cost over twenty-five cents. The material is 100 per cent wool and includes a variety of colors and mixtures, with reds and blues predominating. The only color dyed for the rug was yellow, which was scarce.

LACING WITH NYLON HOSIERY

This method is convenient, inexpensive, and practical, besides being easier on the hands than lacing with stiff linen thread. The hosiery can be very sheer but should not be too old since very old hosiery won't withstand the strain of taut lacing. Once the rug is laced, however, the lacing receives very little wear or strain. Seamless hose is ideal. Discard the tops and feet and cut the stockings in 2- or 3-inch bands, crosswise. Stretch the bands, then interloop 3 or 4 bands, making perhaps a 3-foot-long lacing thread.

HOW TO HANDLE LARGE RUGS

Many people find it easiest to work on the floor when the rug is large, but some women find it impossible to work in this manner. Another way to handle a large braided rug is to keep it half rolled up as you work, with the unrolled part nearest you. A large table or a table with a large piece of plywood on top is the best place to work, with the rolled part on the table. However, a bed can also be a satisfactory surface on which to rest the un-rolled part as you work.

Lace generously as you proceed with a large rug. This is the best assur-ance of a flat rug. Most cupped rugs result from overtight lacing. Any little ripples usually flatten nicely, but if rippling is more than slight, or if there is cupping, it may be necessary to undo a few rows of lacing and rework. Rippling indicates that the work should be tighter; cupping indi-cates that it should be looser.

DETERMINING THE LENGTH OF THE CENTER BRAID

The difference between the length and width of your finished rug will be the length of your basic center braid. To be even more exact, however, add one inch to the center braid, since that is approximately the amount lost in the braiding process. The center, therefore, of a 9 by 12 foot rug would be 3 feet and 1 inch or slightly more. The center of an 8 by 10 foot rug would be a little more than 2 feet.

FINISHING OFF THE BRAIDED RUG

Taper about 12 inches of cables to very fine points. Braid the cables, allowing one of them to extend 2 or 3 inches beyond the end of the braid. Sew the braid securely at the end, and then very tightly lace it onto the rug, stretching the braid as you lace. Lace back and forth until the thread is used up. Pull the one longer cable through a loop just beyond the end. Pull this end very tightly, since this will make a smoother finish for your rug.

BRAIDED BORDERS

Allow about 1½ inches for the width of each row when planning coloring, since the usually recommended cable size for braiding is ¾ inch. Therefore, a 9-inch border requires 6 rows of braiding, a 12-inch border requires 9 rows, and so forth. The larger the rug is, the wider the border should be.

FLOOR MARGINS

Do allow for pleasing floor margins when making room-size braided or hooked rugs. Many think that rugs should be as large as possible, but all handmade rugs are best set off with suitable margins of polished floor. A 12-inch margin is a popular width, but the margin may be 9 or even 6 inches if desired. If the room is very large a margin of 18 inches is acceptable.

57

FURTHER HELP ON TEACHING RUG CLASSES

A semblance of tranquillity is as much a must in rug classes as in any other type of class. Continuous noise produces fatigue and prevents concentration, both of which reduce efficiency. Individuals exposed to loud noises for a long period become jumpy and irritable. Pleasant conversations among friends are fine, but sometimes they get out of hand. An occasional reminder can work wonders.

Political and religious discussions seldom add to the purpose of the class, nor do discussions of personal problems, which should be minimized or, better, omitted. Every teacher no doubt will agree that, although it is sometimes difficult to achieve, the class atmosphere should be friendly, cheerful, and relaxed, yet busy.

Coffee breaks should be allowed, but not mandatory, since some require them, while others prefer to continue with their work. Even if no coffee is consumed, the relaxing interlude promotes better work in many.

Encourage each student to select a permanent spot for working. This will save confusion and ruffled feelings later. Close friends should be able to depend on sitting together, without fear of losing their places should they come late. It is important to the class that people who get along well with each other group together.

Always have extra hooks and scissors available for those who have lost or forgotten their own. However, you should encourage students always to have an extra hook and pair of scissors of their own on hand.

Time can be saved in individual lessons within a class if each member is required to have a box of crayons, a pencil, and a notebook. The teacher can then quickly outline exact places for highlights and shadows, without having to carry her own crayons around the room. Sometimes a rough, quick drawing done in a notebook and shaded with crayons saves repetition of instructions.

Rationing your time fairly among students and retaining complete harmony at the same time is quite an art. Certainly the teacher must be good-natured, for, even though ruggers are usually wonderful to work with, she is certain to have bad moments. The author always concerns herself first with beginners, for they are most likely to need reassurance, and the sooner the better. It is important that they busy themselves as soon as possible, and keep busy. While demonstrating hooking technique or floral shading to one, have other beginners watch too. Until individual instructions in shading are offered, let the beginners practice hooking loops outside their pattern, since some have great difficulty at the beginning.

After the beginner gets busy, then it is a good idea to give your attention to the in-between people who have had experience but don't yet qualify as experts. Their lessons are somewhat briefer than those for beginners, since they understand rug language. They are more likely to have such problems as choosing colors for their designs or backgrounds, for which a few words from the teacher will be sufficient. If one student's lesson is of group interest, others should stand by and listen. Beginners can pick up valuable pointers this way.

Expert class members should usually be the last in line for help. They are always understanding, but perhaps their patience can be rewarded by allowing a little extra time for the more intricate lessons. These members afford real class inspiration, for to beginners, their work is beyond reproach.

After classes are going smoothly a good way of proving impartiality among students is to conduct classes on a first come, first serve basis. No one can argue with this method of instruction, since it emphasizes fairness as well as encourages students to get to class on time. Too, a change in methods of conducting classes adds to class interest.

The student who insists on attention before his turn is a problem faced by every teacher sooner or later. Unfortunately, good-natured teachers are often imposed upon by such students. These overzealous students should be discouraged as much as possible, but because we are teaching adults much tact and diplomacy is called for. Sometimes a yes or no suffices, but other times the situation is troublesome. One solution is to explain ahead of time the undesirability of helping students out of turn, and adding that when, under certain circumstances, a student is helped out of turn, she must be content with a short turn. Class dignity is thus retained in an otherwise tense or embarrassing situation. It requires diplomacy, to say the least.

The study of human behavior can be extremely helpful to the teacher of rugmaking. A course in psychology is therefore recommended. Libraries also can offer many books on the subject of human behavior, which is sure to prove very interesting, as well as helpful, in the teaching of adults. A teacher who has the knack of keeping class harmony and good will, however otherwise qualified or unqualified she may be, has an important asset which will always help her in teaching.

The author strongly recommends college courses on the techniques of teaching adults. For instance, courses on audio-visual techniques and even on parent education can be invaluable.

A great deal of interest can be added to a class by field trips to see art exhibits, class exhibits, or even homes that contain many handworked articles. Visits to other classes can inspire your students, as can authorities on particular facets of rugmaking who are invited as speakers to your own classes.

Check to see if your library has an adult-services librarian with specific responsibility for the library's adult-education activities. A class visit to the library or library research assignments may benefit the students. The library is an excellent source of pictures and magazine articles and books pertaining to rug work. Many libraries have films, records, and slides related to rugmaking. If your library is not large enough to have such articles, perhaps it can borrow them from another library.

58

HOOKING AND BRAIDING HINTS

DESIGNS AND DESIGN SOURCES

- Collect autumn leaves for copying later. Preserve their colors by placing them in a cardboard box and alternating layers of leaves with layers of borax. Let them stand 2 or 3 days. Shake off the borax and wipe each leaf with liquid wax.
- Another way to preserve leaves for later copying is to press perfect specimens flat and then cover them with clear, self-adhesive plastic. This will protect their color and shape.
- Include various juvenile books on your reference shelf. They include a wide variety of subjects and their pictures are drawn and colored simply. Especially recommended are the following Golden Books: *My Little Golden Dictionary, The Golden Book of Flowers,* and *A Day on the Farm.*
- Old embroidery direction books are very helpful in shading hooked flowers and leaves.
- The following back issues of *National Geographic Magazine* are very good sources of design: September 1951 ("How Fruit Came to America"—includes 26 illustrations and 24 paintings); July 1947 ("The World Is Your Garden"—includes 10 flower illustrations and 24 paintings of flowers).
- Your local public library undoubtedly has many books with usable designs.

- An impressive, but fairly easy, rug pattern is a map of all the states. Add part of Canada and Mexico and hook state flowers in each state, with maple leaf for Canada and cactus for Mexico.
- A pine-cone design makes an attractive woodbox seat.
- Ten-cent stores contain limitless design inspiration in the form of such articles as decals, greeting cards, handkerchiefs, place mats, shelf paper, oilcloth, seed packages, embroidered items, china, and waste baskets.

SPOTTING AND TOUCHING-UP

- Toothpicks are good for spotting leftover windows in hooking. Just place toothpicks through the back side, then turn rug over, finish filling in, and remove toothpick.
- Touching-up or replacing some coloring may require aging the new material to match. Try exposing such material to the sunlight for a while until it takes on the softer hue that time produces in all hooked coloring.
- To revive an old hooked rug, dilute different color dyes in separate cups of hot water, dampen design with hot water, then paint dissolved colorings on with a brush.
- To touch up the sky of a hooked picture, use ordinary blue crayon, making light strokes until the desired tone is obtained. Some streakiness will make the sky all the more effective. For a sunset sky, use orange and yellow crayons near the horizon and change gradually to softer yellows and blues above.

CARE AND STORAGE OF RUGS

- To mothproof woolens, add 1 tablespoon of turpentine for each 1½ pounds of wool to rinse water when washing them.
- For tieing up a rolled-rug, use old nylon hosiery instead of string.
- To discourage moths in closets, fill with whole cloves small bags made from a thin material and place them on coat hangers or hooks.
- Cashmere woolens should be given special care since they have a particular attraction for moths and silverfish.
- Small braided rugs can be beautifully washed in the washing machine (with the dial set for modern fabrics). Dry them on a flat surface after shaping them. Never wash hooked rugs in a machine because it causes burlap to deteriorate.
- Store woolens or finished hooked pieces in plastic bags made airtight with foil. Tear off a 2-inch strip of household foil and fold it in half lengthwise. Fit the folded strip over the open end of plastic bag holding item to be stored. Set iron for medium heat (wool setting). Quickly run tip (about ½ inch) of iron across foil strip. Let it cool, lift off foil. Bag can be resealed in same way after opening.

- To stop rug-end raveling on a worn hooked rug, mix together until smooth equal parts of plain gelatin and boiling water. Apply mixture to back side of rug with a brush.
- To avoid friction wear from a television set on a large rug, place a smaller rug over the large one.

EQUIPMENT AND SUPPLIES

- To sharpen shears, cut through sandpaper or run blades across the neck of a bottle as though you were cutting off the bottle neck.
- If your rug hook becomes dull or overly difficult to push through burlap mesh, sharpen it on an emery board or the striking strip of a match cover.
- Protect your rug book with a piece of glass placed over the open pages when you are referring to it while dyeing.
- Scotch tape a sheet of plastic around the cover of your rug book to keep it looking like new.
- Another way to keep your rug book clean when checking directions while dyeing is to clamp a trouser hanger over the top of the opened book and hang it from a cupboard door.
- Hookers who use a stapler to attach a pattern to a frame say it is far superior to thumbtacks. A regular-size hand stapler which can be opened flat is the type needed.
- A stapler can also be used to refasten swatch strips together after you cut off what you need.
- Save time when making cables for braiding by using a stapler to hold folds in place. Immediately after braiding remove the staples that show.
- A plate easel is perfect for holding a picture that you are copying. Small, curved shears, especially made for hooking, are almost essential for convenience and best results. They are lighter in weight than regular shears and their points can be used for all kinds of shaping and molding.
- Magnigrips, small magnets, attached to the pattern are another convenient way to hold hook and small scissors when not in use.
- A discarded faucet handle can be made into a hand lightweight hammer for pounding thumbtacks into frames. First blunt one end and then attach a wooden handle.
- The foam-rubber tape now available has adhesive backing that sticks to metal, glass, wood, or fabrics. Used on the backs of rugs, it prevents their slipping on the floor. It can also be used for taping over old rug frames that are rough and splintery.

DYEING

- To save time in dyeing a color series, first dye the strips without using salt or vinegar, taking only about 5 or 6 minutes for 6 shades. Rinse the strips slightly, and then set colors by placing all 6 at one time in boiling water to which vinegar has been added. Simmer them for about 5 minutes, then rinse.

- Khaki-color woolens overdyed with purples results in pretty brown tones. Some red dye warms the results if you prefer a richer brown.
- Widen your hooking horizon by dyeing swatches of such colors as gray, brown, mahogany, spice, brandy, navy blue. Even a series dyed from black can yield beautiful violet-blue shades that are perfect for unusual daisies, etc.
- To darken bronze green, when dyeing, try adding a bit of mahogany dye, for a rich, dark shade.
- A trick of darkening yellow material without losing any of the pretty yellow coloring is to use a weak dye bath with taupe dye. It softens the yellow brightness perfectly.
- More lasting than other blues is a combination of royal blue and sky blue, according to one chemical company. Other colors with tendencies to fade such as yellows and golds, should be allowed to simmer in the dye for a longer time to acquire colorfastness.
- Unless otherwise directed, add salt directly after the wet woolen is placed in the dye bath and stirred. Salt is simmered in just as long as woolen is dyed, which ensures lasting quality.
- Green dye over gray material produces a blue-green, just as green dye over beige produces shades leaning toward bronze greens. This must be considered when dyeing. Only white material will produce the true coloring of the dye used.
- Before dyeing, wet your woolens in water with detergent and do not rinse them. This will make the woolens dye more easily and quickly.

COLORS

- A spray of gray leaves in a floral grouping can be very pretty.
- In hooking an ear of corn, try making Indian corn, using dashes of purple, ivory, yellow, and gray, in short rows throughout the ear.
- A gold scroll, outlined with a brown-check wool, is especially effective against a light background.
- Plums and cherries always appear more realistic with a white highlight.
- The best shadow lining for a flower is usually the darkest color used in the flower, done very finely, in a hit-or-miss outline, if background is light. If background is dark, outline with the lightest color. A cocoa shade affords sufficient contrast for a light beige background.

GIFTS

- In giving a hooked gift, why not include a case history of the article, describing the number of hours, days, or months spent, and other interesting or amusing anecdotes and facts that happened during its making? You can also include the identity of the material used, if of interest, such as dad's pants, baby's blanket, or mother's coat. Attach the case history in a small pocket attached to the reverse side of the hooked article, preferably near a corner. Let it be a surprise.

- For gifts of hooked pictures, Victorian busts of a lady and gentleman are popular, and each can be finished in two or three hours. Other subjects are animals, birds, flowers, fruits, etc. The design should be simple and uncluttered on decorator burlap. Leave the background unworked, since the burlap texture is very attractive when the picture is framed.

CLASSES IN RUGMAKING

- If you are a teacher, you might try appealing to braiders to bring their leftovers into class for hookers, who find good uses for all manner of odds and ends.
- If you need just a few credits for a high school diploma, you may find that credits for a rug-making class count. Why not check into this?
- Many inquire how to obtain accredited teaching credentials of rug classes. In most states it is quite simple. Here are the procedures in California as an example: First, attend an accredited rug class in Adult Education. Then take the state-required course in Adult Methods and Procedures in any subject offered by certain colleges. You will need 4 credits for a two-year teaching certificate. Next, contact a Principal of Adult Education who needs a rug teacher. He is the one to send your application to the proper state agency along with his recommendation. After this is processed, your credentials are registered locally by his office, and you receive your assignment.
- Instead of the teacher answering all class problems, why not make them class solutions instead? Let class members each have a voice as the more important questions come up, so each may benefit.

GENERAL HINTS

- To use a rug in a hallway that is narrower than the rug, turn one side of the rug under to make the rug fit, then cut down the pad underneath the rug to accommodate the fold of the rug.
- Make hallway runners in two or more pieces, instead of one, in case you ever wish to use them as separate rugs instead of as a single runner.
- Always use nonskid pads under small rugs to prevent accidents.
- In cutting strips for the background of a hooked rug, 5/32 inch is usually wide enough, but ⅛-inch strips may be required for heavier, stiffer material.
- When adding braiding around a hooked rug, use the 1-inch or the 1½-

inch braiders. These make sheer braids just about the same thickness as that of a hooked rug.

- The 1- or 1½-inch braiders are also good for kitchen or bathroom rugs, since the extra thinness of the braids makes it easier to wash the rugs.
- If two colors or kinds of material are used to begin a braided rug instead of three, form the T by attaching the second color strip to the center of a longer strip of the first color, thus forming the three ends for braiding.
- Picture hooking may require 3/32-inch strips or ⅛-inch strips, depending on the type of design and on the weave and weight of wool used.
- "Seasoning" a hooked rug has been claimed to be of great benefit—at least to the maker. When you finish a rug, roll it up and place it in a closet for three months. It is guaranteed that at the end of that time you will be far more receptive to its beauty.
- Old dress gloves can make braiding much easier on the hands.
- In working through double seams of a spliced pattern, take time out to pull out some of the selvage thread. It makes seams twice as easy to hook through.
- If you do hooking in the evening, it is wise to select your colors during the daytime.
- Instead of trimming off excess burlap from a hooked picture when framing it, fold the burlap back, press it flat, and, for extra neatness, sew it down on the back side. You will welcome this extra burlap later if you ever decide to convert the picture into something else, such as a chair seat, which may require a larger pattern.
- For decorator results, make sure that your hooked pictures are hung absolutely flat, and hang them so that the center is at eye level of a standing person.
- Hooked pictures for which it is difficult to find the right shape frames without undue expense can be easily mounted as a grouping on plywood or cardboard. Such a grouped wall hanging can be very attractive.
- To plan your picture grouping before hanging the pictures, cut a sheet of butcher's paper or other heavy-duty paper to the size of the wall area and place the pictures on the paper in the desired position. Outline the pictures and tape the paper to the wall. Then lightly hammer nails into marked positions.
- Odd pieces of burlap from mother's work may afford much pleasure to children, especially little girls handy with a sewing needle. Designs in colored yarns on burlap make a big hit.
- Watch for sales of framed pictures in local stores. Many frames make it well worth while to discard their current picture. Natural wood unfinished frames from ten-cent stores are popular.
- Tie a strip around cut strips of the same shades while you are hooking. This will keep the different shades separated.

- Use safety pins for pinning excess burlap out of the way while working on a pattern. To prevent snagging the burlap with the pins put a button on the pin before pinning through the burlap and then put another button on before shutting the pin.

AVAILABILITY OF PATTERNS SHOWN

Most of the patterns shown in this book are available through the following address:

Hooker's Guild
Box 43012, La Tijera Station
Los Angeles 43, California

The author may also be reached through the above address. Your questions and comments are always welcome.

Index

INDEX

National Geographic Magazine, as design
source, 268
Neal, K., 57
needlepoint, as design source, 56
needles:
    for braided rugs, 186–187
    for combination rugs, 194
    see also hooks
neutral colors:
    in backgrounds, 91, 125, 126, 129
    in braided rugs, 191
    for flowers, 97
New England, rug hooking in, 9
nineteenth century rugs, 11, 12
nosegay patterns, 127, 130, 160
nursery designs, 152, 154, 155
nylon hosiery, lacing with, 260, 263

oak leaves, 226, 227–228
oblong rugs, border of, 194–195
open-petal flower pattern, 59–62
orange, overdyeing of, 92
organdy method, of pattern transfer, 215
Oriental design, 29, 154
oval rugs:
    braided, 185–187
    combination, 194–195
    with fruit design, 164
overdyeing, 91–92

pads, for rugs, 196, 199, 272
paintbrush dyeing, 234–235
painted scrolls, 243
pansies:
    coloring for, 97, 225
    patterns, 76–78
paper, for patterns, 45, 47, 215
pastels, 20
    for backgrounds, 127, 129, 134, 242
    for borders, 135
patterns:
    address for, 275
    animal, 153, 154, 155
    attaching of, 22–24, 169
    block, see block patterns
    for chair seats, 165–169
    color guide on, 82–83
    for combination rugs, 192, 195
    commercial, 14, 161, 164
    enlarging of, 152–154
    flower, see floral patterns
    for footstools, 165–169
    frame for, 15
    Frost stencils for, 10
    fruit, 112–117
    leaf, 71–73, 78–80, 108
    making of, 41–47, 139–141
    scrolls in, 119–120, 122, 125
    sources of, 139, 152, 275
    in teaching hooking, 208, 265, 266

patterns (cont.)
    transfer of, 45, 47, 215
    see also design
peaches, 104, 223
pears, 104, 116–118
petals:
    pansy, 76, 78, 225
    rose, 63, 65–66
    shading of, 60–62, 222
picture hooking, 170–176, 273
    frames, 175–176, 251, 273
    ideas for, 247–251
    material for, 171–172, 213
    touching-up, 269
pineapples, coloring for, 224
pine cones, 226
pine needles, 226
pink:
    in color series for grapes, 98
    in dyeing, 92, 93, 103
plaids, 19–20, 218
    for borders, 134, 243
    for braiding, 262–263
    for flower centers, 60, 67, 69, 70, 225,
        244
    for scrolls, 121, 122, 242, 243–244
plums:
    dyeing for, 104, 237
    shading of, 116–117, 271
poinsettia rug, 32
poppies, dyes for, 97
portraits, in hooked pictures, 249–251
pressing, of rug, 50, 53
prices, for hooked rugs, 203–204
primitive design, 152, 154
punchwork rugs, 19, 24
    see also yarn
purple:
    in color series for grapes, 98
    in overdyeing, 92
    in continuity dyeing, 236

quilts, as design source, 52, 132, 151

red:
    barn, 214
    bleaching of, 89–90
    in color scheme, 82
    dyeing for, 95–96
    in overdyeing, 92
    for scrolls, 242
regal lilies, 97
rocking chairs, covers for, 166–167, 213–
    214
roll method, of spot dyeing, 233
rosebuds, 66–67
rose color:
    in backgrounds, 128, 241–242
    in scrolls, 125, 127, 134
Rose and Iris rug, 64

Rose and Lily, 160
roses:
  color series for, 63, 65–68, 89–90
  dyes for, 97, 238–239
  heraldic, 145
  hooking of, 63–68, 222
  leaves for, 97, 104, 109
  patterns, 63–68, 86, 145
  talisman, 239
  yellow, 238
Roses and Buds rug, 123
rug frames, see frames, rug
rugs:
  braided, see braided rugs
  care of, 196–199, 258–259, 269–270
  combination, 192–195, 272–273
  display of, 253–254
  hooked, see hooking
  marketing of, 200–204
  room-size, handling of, 255–256, 263
  shapes of, 141, 185–186, 203
  value of, 203–204

samplers, hooking of, 252
Sattelkau, Ruth, 58
Scandinavia, rug hooking from, 9
scenic rugs, use of, 253–254
scissors, 21, 270
  support for, 138
scrapbooks, for designs, 55–56, 207
scrolls:
  colors for, 119–125, 127, 134, 242–244,
    271
  dyeing methods for, 99, 232, 233
  in eighteenth-century design, 161, 162
  and floral center, 49, 50
  patterns, 52, 53, 120, 122, 125, 162
  types of, 119–124
  in Victorian design, 131, 164
seat covers, 157, 165–169, 257, 261
seed packages, as design source, 55
selling, of rugs, 200–204
Seven Iris rug, 124
shading:
  fingering in, 74–80
  in layers, see color series
shadowing, 59, 118, 128–129, 271
shapes:
  of braided rugs, 185–186
  of rugs, 141
  for salable rugs, 203
Sharp, Mrs. B. H., 57
short-handle hook, 13, 18–19, 23
  use of, 35–40, 48–53
Shunk, Mrs. Shirley, 54
signature, on hooked pieces, 175, 245
simmering, bleaching by, 90
sizes:
  of rugs, 141, 152, 185

sizes (cont.)
  for salable rugs, 203
sizing, of yarn rug, 31
Slater, Joseph, 146, 147
Sleigh Ride, The, 173
solvents, rug-cleaning, 197–198
space skipping, 38
Spencer, Clara, 123
spirals, for grape clusters, 98
spot-dyed strips:
  hooking with, 107–109, 174
  for signature and date, 245
spot dyeing, 101–104
  for fruits, 104, 223–224
  roll method of, 233
spots, removal of, 259
spotting, 269
Spring Blossoms print, 247
stair carpets, 152, 157, 159
  as combination rug, 192, 193
Stanick, Opal and Charles, 88
stapler, use of, 270
Star Compass rug, 147
stems:
  fern, 73
  fruit, 98, 112–117
stool covers, 165–166
  braided, 260–261
storing, of rugs, 199, 259, 269
strawberries, shading of, 114
strips:
  for braiding, 183–184
  see also cut strips
sunsets, in hooked pictures, 249, 269

talisman roses, 239
tan:
  for backgrounds, 20, 91, 126
  for borders, 135
Taubes, Frederic, 176
teaching, of rug hooking, 205–208, 265–
  267, 272
Three Fishes rug, 146
Tiger Lily rug, 142
touching-up, 269
transfer, of design, 45, 47, 215
trees, in hooked pictures, 247
trellis scroll, 160
tulips:
  dyes for, 97
  patterns, 71, 72
turns, in hooking, 39–40
tweeds, 19–20
  in hooked pictures, 247

Ulmann, Bernhard, Co., 33, 106

vacuum cleaning, for rugs, 196, 258–259
value, of hooked rugs, 203–204
Van Wyck, Kathleen, 64, 77